TEACHER'S PET PUBLICATIONS

LITPLAN TEACHER PACK
for
Cry, the Beloved Country
based on the book by
Alan Paton

Written by
Mary B. Collins

© 1996 Teacher's Pet Publications
All Rights Reserved

This **LitPlan** for Alan Paton's
Cry, the Beloved Country
has been brought to you by Teacher's Pet Publications, Inc.

Copyright Teacher's Pet Publications 1996

Only the student materials in this unit plan
such as worksheets, study questions, assignment sheets, and tests
may be reproduced multiple times for use in the purchaser's classroom.

For any additional copyright questions,
contact Teacher's Pet Publications.

www.tpet.com

TABLE OF CONTENTS - *Cry, the Beloved Country*

Introduction	5
Unit Objectives	7
Reading Assignment Sheet	8
Unit Outline	9
Study Questions (Short Answer)	13
Quiz/Study Questions (Multiple Choice)	24
Pre-reading Vocabulary Worksheets	43
Lesson One (Introductory Lesson)	57
Nonfiction Assignment Sheet	59
Oral Reading Evaluation Form	65
Writing Assignment 1	62
Writing Assignment 2	67
Writing Assignment 3	73
Writing Evaluation Form	75
Vocabulary Review Activities	71
Extra Writing Assignments/Discussion ?s	69
Unit Review Activities	79
Unit Tests	83
Unit Resource Materials	113
Vocabulary Resource Materials	127

A FEW NOTES ABOUT THE AUTHOR
Alan Paton

ALAN PATON was born in 1903 in Pietermaritzburg, South Africa. In 1922 he graduated from the University of Natal with a degree in mathematics (and later a second degree in education). Beginning in 1925 he taught at a native school in Ixopo, and following that he became principal of Diepkloof Reformatory (for boys.

After World War II, he began studying prisons and reformatories, traveled to the United States, England, Canada and Sweden. While on this trip he got the idea for *Cry, the Beloved Country*, which was published in 1948.

Some of Alan Paton's other works are *Too Late the Phalarope* (1953), *The Land and the People of South Africa* (1955), *Hope for South Africa* (1959), *Tales From a Troubled Land* (1961), *Debbie Go Home* (1961), and *Ah, But Your Land Is Beautiful* (1982).

INTRODUCTION

This unit has been designed to develop students' reading, writing, thinking, and language skills through exercises and activities related to *Cry, the Beloved Country* by Alan Paton. It includes twenty lessons, supported by extra resource materials.

In the **introductory lesson** students are given the materials they will be using during the unit. At the end of the lesson, students begin the pre-reading work for the first reading assignment.

In addition, there is a **nonfiction reading assignment**. Students are required to read two pieces of nonfiction related in some way to *Cry, the Beloved Country*. After reading their nonfiction pieces, students will fill out a worksheet on which they answer questions regarding facts, interpretation, criticism, and personal opinions. During two class periods, students make **oral presentations** about the nonfiction pieces they have read. This not only exposes all students to a wealth of information, it also gives students the opportunity to practice **public speaking**.

The **reading assignments** are approximately thirty pages each; some are a little shorter while others are a little longer. Students have approximately 15 minutes of pre-reading work to do prior to each reading assignment. This pre-reading work involves reviewing the study questions for the assignment and doing some vocabulary work for 8 to 10 vocabulary words they will encounter in their reading.

The **study guide questions** are fact-based questions; students can find the answers to these questions right in the text. These questions come in two formats: short answer required or multiple choice. The best use of these materials is probably to use the short answer version of the questions as study guides for students (since answers will be more complete), and to use the multiple choice version for occasional quizzes. If your school has the appropriate equipment, it might be a good idea to make transparencies of your answer keys for the overhead projector.

The **vocabulary work** is intended to enrich students' vocabularies as well as to aid in the students' understanding of the book. Prior to each reading assignment, students will complete a two-part worksheet for approximately 8 to 10 vocabulary words in the upcoming reading assignment. Part I focuses on students' use of general knowledge and contextual clues by giving the sentence in which the word appears in the text. Students are then to write down what they think the words mean based on the words' usage. Part II nails down the definitions of the words by giving students dictionary definitions of the words and having students match the words to the correct definitions based on the words' contextual usage. Students should then have a good understanding of the words when they meet them in the text.

After each reading assignment, students will go back and formulate answers for the study guide questions. Discussion of these questions serves as a **review** of the most important events and ideas presented in the reading assignments.

After students complete reading the work, there is a **vocabulary review** lesson which pulls together all of the fragmented vocabulary lists for the reading assignments and gives students a review of all of the words they have studied.

A lesson is devoted to the **extra discussion questions/writing assignments**. These questions focus on interpretation, critical analysis and personal response, employing a variety of thinking skills and adding to the students' understanding of the novel.

The **group activity** which follows the discussion questions has students working together to create a film about South Africa using all the information they have gathered through the nonfiction reading assignment, the reading and discussion of the book, and the writing assignments.

There are three **writing assignments** in this unit, each with the purpose of informing, persuading, or having students express personal opinions. The first assignment is to inform: in preparation for the oral presentations students make a written composition telling the facts from the nonfiction articles they have read. The second assignment is to express personal opinions: students create five questions requiring an opinion for an answer and interview three of their classmates. Following the interviews, students write a composition telling about all the different answers they received in the interviews. The third assignment is to persuade: students write the script for a commercial relating to South Africa -- a public service commercial against apartheid, a commercial from a South African manufacturer advertising products, or some other commercial the student creates related to South Africa and the material covered in class.

The **review lesson** pulls together all of the aspects of the unit. The teacher is given four or five choices of activities or games to use which all serve the same basic function of reviewing all of the information presented in the unit.

The **unit test** comes in two formats: all multiple choice-matching-true/false or with a mixture of matching, short answer, multiple choice, and composition. As a convenience, two different tests for each format have been included.

There are additional **support materials** included with this unit. The **extra activities section** includes suggestions for an in-class library, crossword and word search puzzles related to the novel, and extra vocabulary worksheets. There is a list of **bulletin board ideas** which gives the teacher suggestions for bulletin boards to go along with this unit. In addition, there is a list of **extra class activities** the teacher could choose from to enhance the unit or as a substitution for an exercise the teacher might feel is inappropriate for his/her class. **Answer keys** are located directly after the **reproducible student materials** throughout the unit. The student materials may be reproduced for use in the teacher's classroom without infringement of copyrights. No other portion of this unit may be reproduced without the written consent of Teacher's Pet Publications, Inc.

UNIT OBJECTIVES - *Cry, the Beloved Country*

1. Through reading Paton's *Cry, the Beloved Country*, students will better understand the country and people of South Africa.

2. Students will demonstrate their understanding of the text on four levels: factual, interpretive, critical and personal.

3. To show students that racial conflicts, social injustices and problems with crime exist in other countries; they are problems caused by people, not geographical boundaries.

4. Students will see that each of our daily life experiences changes us and shapes our thoughts and feelings.

5. Students will be given the opportunity to practice reading aloud and silently to improve their skills in each area.

6. Students will answer questions to demonstrate their knowledge and understanding of the main events and characters in *Cry, the Beloved Country* as they relate to the author's theme development.

7. Students will enrich their vocabularies and improve their understanding of the novel through the vocabulary lessons prepared for use in conjunction with the novel.

8. The writing assignments in this unit are geared to several purposes:
    a. To have students demonstrate their abilities to inform, to persuade, or to express their own personal ideas
        Note: Students will demonstrate ability to write effectively to <u>inform</u> by developing and organizing facts to convey information. Students will demonstrate the ability to write effectively to <u>persuade</u> by selecting and organizing relevant information, establishing an argumentative purpose, and by designing an appropriate strategy for an identified audience. Students will demonstrate the ability to write effectively to <u>express personal ideas</u> by selecting a form and its appropriate elements.
    b. To check the students' reading comprehension
    c. To make students think about the ideas presented by the novel
    d. To encourage logical thinking
    e. To provide an opportunity to practice good grammar and improve students' use of the English language.

9. Students will read aloud, report, and participate in large and small group discussions to improve their public speaking and personal interaction skills.

READING ASSIGNMENT SHEET - *Cry, the Beloved Country*

Date Assigned	Chapters Assigned	Completion Date
	1-5	
	6-7	
	8-10	
	11-14	
	15-17	
	18-21	
	22-29	
	30-36	

UNIT OUTLINE - *Cry, the Beloved Country*

1	2	3	4	5
Introduction PVR 1-5	Study ?s 1-5 Library	Writing Assignment #1 PVR 6-7	Study ?s 6-7 Reports PVR 8-10	Reports
6	**7**	**8**	**9**	**10**
Study ?s 8-10 Reports PVR 11-14	Study ?s 11-14 PVR 15-17	Study ?s 15-17 Writing Assignment #2 PVR 18-21	Study ?s 18-21 PVR 22-29	Study?s 22-29 PVR 30-36
11	**12**	**13**	**14**	**15**
Study?s 30-36 Extra ?s	Vocabulary	Writing Assignment #3	Project	Project
16	**17**	**18**	**19**	**20**
Project	Filming	View Film	Review	Test

Key: P=Preview Study Questions V=Prereading Vocabulary Worksheet R=Read

STUDY GUIDE QUESTIONS

SHORT ANSWER STUDY GUIDE QUESTIONS - *Cry, the Beloved Country*

Chapters 1 - 5
1. Paragraphs two and three in Chapter 1 sharply contrast. Explain the significance of these two paragraphs in terms of the novel's central theme. (Come back to this later if you can't answer it at first.)
2. Identify Stephen, John, and Gertrude.
3. "Once such a thing is opened, it cannot be shut again." Explain.
4. Why did Stephen Kumalo go to Johannesburg?
5. "The lights . . . fall . . . on the grass and stones of a country that sleeps." Explain the symbolic significance of this statement.
6. What does "Umfundisi" mean?
7. "The journey had begun. And now the fear back again . . . ." What fears did Kumalo have?
8. What happened to Kumalo when he first arrived in Johannesburg?
9. Identify Msimangu and Mrs. Lithebe.
10. Describe Gertrude's sickness.
11. Why is Gertrude's sickness upsetting to Kumalo?
12. What is Kumalo's brother John doing in Johannesburg?
13. "The tragedy is not that things are broken. The tragedy is that they are not mended again." Explain what Msimangu meant.
14. "It is fear that rules this land." Who fears whom?

Chapters 6 & 7
1. Describe Kumalo's meeting with his sister (when he finds her in Johannesburg).
2. Kumalo bought Gertrude and the child new clothes. Why is that symbolically important?
3. Describe Kumalo's first meeting with his brother John in Johannesburg.
4. What is Msimangu's one hope for his country?

Chapters 8 - 10
1. Why did Dubauwoodnt Kumalo ask Msimangu to walk instead of taking a bus?
2. Why is the government more afraid of Dubula than Tomlinson or John Kumalo?
3. What did Mrs. Mkize tell them about Absalom?
4. What is the point of Chapter 9 in relationship to the novel's themes?
5. When Kumalo finally reached Pimville, where Absalom was supposed to be living, what did he find?

Cry Beloved Short Answer Study Questions Page 2

Chapters 11 - 14
1. A certain news headline and article grabbed the attention of the priests at the Mission House. What was the article about?
2. Identify James and Arthur Jarvis.
3. "Cry, the beloved country, these things are not yet at an end." What "things"?
4. "There are voices crying what must be done, a hundred, a thousand voices." Chapter 12 gives several examples of what these "voices" say. What <u>do</u> they say?
5. What news of Absalom does Mrs. Ndlela give Msimangu?
6. To what decisions did Kumalo come in Ezenzeleni?
7. Where does Kumalo finally meet Absalom? Describe their meeting.
8. How does John decide to handle his son's defense?

Chapters 15 - 17
1. What is Father Vincent's gift to Kumalo?
2. Why does Father Vincent say sorrow is better than fear?
3. In what way was Kumalo cruel to the girl?
4. To what arrangement do Kumalo and the girl finally agree?
5. Describe the content of the conversation between Mrs. Lithebe and the girl.
6. Identify Mr. Carmichael.

Chapters 18 - 21
1. Book II begins with the same sentence as Book I did. Compare and contrast the beginning passages of Book I and Book II.
2. Contrast Jarvis' arrival in Johannesburg with Kumalo's.
3. What was ironic about Arthur Jarvis' death?
4. Why did Arthur Jarvis read about Lincoln?
5. What were Arthur Jarvis' last written words?

Chapters 22 - 25
1. Explain the difference between "justice" and "just."
2. "No second Johannesburg is needed upon the earth. One is enough." Explain why not.
3. Why was Jarvis "sick at heart" as he read some of his son's papers?
4. Why did Kumalo appear to be ill when Jarvis opened the door?
5. What was Jarvis' reaction after Kumalo identified himself as the father of his son's murderer?

Cry Beloved Short Answer Study Questions Page 3

Chapters 26 - 29
1. "There is no applause in prison." Explain the inference regarding John Kumalo.
2. "Nothing is ever quiet except for fools." Explain.
3. Why was the headline about another housebreak-murder "bad news"?
4. What is the verdict for Absalom?
5. Why did Absalom marry the girl even though he was sentenced to death?
6. Explain the significance of the name of Peter for Absalom's son.
7. Why did Gertrude leave?

Chapters 30 - 32
1. Describe Kumalo's return home.
2. Why did Kumalo visit the chief? What did he want?
3. Who was the small boy who rode to Kumalo's place?
4. What is the significance of the boy's trying to learn Zulu?
5. What was Mr. Jarvis' first gift to the natives of Kumalo's village?

Chapters 33 - 36
1. What was Jarvis' second gift to the natives?
2. Who died?
3. What did Kumalo do for Jarvis? What did the natives do for him?
4. When the Bishop came for the confirmations, what did he suggest for Kumalo?
5. Why was Kumalo not transferred?
6. What happened to Absalom?
7. Why did Kumalo go to the mountain?
8. Explain the significance of the fact that the book ends at sunrise.
9. The last paragraph of the novel speaks of "the fear of bondage and the bondage of fear." Explain the relevance of this phrase.

ANSWER KEY SHORT ANSWER STUDY GUIDE QUESTIONS - *Cry, The Beloved Country*

Chapters 1 - 5

1. Paragraphs two and three in Chapter 1 sharply contrast. Explain the significance of these two paragraphs in terms of the novel's central theme. (Come back to this later if you can't answer it at first.)
    Paton symbolically describes the land. As it was rich and plentiful, the tribe also flourished. As the land became overworked and mistreated, the tribal life failed. The land becomes a symbol of tribal life. Also, as the ruined land is symbolic of the native life, the good lands which hold the water are symbolic of the white man's life. There is a deep contrast between the "haves" and "have nots."

2. Identify Stephen, John, and Gertrude.
    Rev. Stephen Kumalo is the main character of the novel who travels to Johannesburg in hopes of restoring order to his family. John is Stephen's brother. Gertrude is Stephen's sister.

3. "Once such a thing is opened, it cannot be shut again." Explain.
    Stephen Kumalo was reluctant to open the letter in his hands. Such a letter only came with very good or very bad news. Either way, the reader would be irreversibly affected. One may also symbolically infer that once a person is made aware of a problem (such as social injustice) he cannot turn away; the problem will not go away by itself; action must be taken.

4. Why did Stephen Kumalo go to Johannesburg?
    He received a letter informing him that his sister who had moved there was not well. He went to see what he could do for her. While there, he intended to try to find his brother and his son who also had gone to Johannesburg to live.

5. "The lights . . . fall . . . on the grass and stones of a country that sleeps." Explain the symbolic significance of this statement.
    This is another reference to the symbolism used in Chapter 1. The grass could symbolically be whites and the stones could symbolically be natives. Light traditionally symbolizes education or justice; in this case, perhaps it is public awareness. Perhaps all together these images suggest the beginning of a public awareness by both natives and whites that the problems of social injustice cannot be ignored anymore.

6. What does "Umfundisi" mean?
    Umfundisi means pastor or reverend.

7. "The journey had begun. And now the fear back again . . . ." What fears did Kumalo have?
   He had fear of the unknown, fear of a city where boys were killed crossing the street, fear of Gertrude's sickness, fear for his son's well-being, and "deep down the fear of a man who lives in a world not made for him, whose own world is slipping away, dying, being destroyed. . . ."

8. What happened to Kumalo when he first arrived in Johannesburg?
   A young man pretended to help him buy his bus ticket but stole his money.

9. Identify Msimangu and Mrs. Lithebe.
   Msimangu is a reverend who sent for Kumalo and helps him in Johannesburg. Mrs. Lithebe is the woman who rents Kumalo a room.

10. Describe Gertrude's sickness.
    She is morally corrupt. She makes and sells liquor, lives with prostitutes (and we assume she is one), and she has been in prison. It is not a physical sickness that attracts Msimangu's attention, but a moral one.

11. Why is Gertrude's sickness upsetting to Kumalo?
    Being a man of God, immorality in any form is distasteful; however, having his own sister behave this way is truly upsetting. He would hope that his own family would behave in a more God-like fashion.

12. What is Kumalo's brother John doing in Johannesburg?
    He has turned into a politician, speaking in public for the cause of the natives.

13. "The tragedy is not that things are broken. The tragedy is that they are not mended again." Explain what Msimangu meant. (Ch. 5)
    It is bad enough that there is such injustice in South Africa, though one can see how it came about. The wrong comes in that the injustices have not been eliminated since they have been recognized.

14. "It is fear that rules this land." Who fears whom?
    Whites fear the natives and the natives fear the whites.

Chapters 6 & 7
1. Describe Kumalo's meeting with his sister (when he finds her in Johannesburg).
   He confronts her with each of his questions--why she didn't write, if she found her husband, that she was in prison, etc. She answers simply and truthfully. Their first minutes together seem cool--not at all the warm embrace one might think brother and sister might share. The relationship doesn't begin to warm up until she agrees to leave Johannesburg with Kumalo.

2. Kumalo bought Gertrude and the child new clothes. Why is that symbolically important?
   The new clothes symbolize the putting on of a new life.

3. Describe Kumalo's first meeting with his brother John in Johannesburg.
   Kumalo confronts him just as he did his sister. Notice, though, that John's answers come with long qualifiers and explanations (unlike Gertrude's).

4. What is Msimangu's one hope for his country?
   He hopes that one day "white men and black men, desiring neither power or money, but desiring only the good of their country, come together to work for it."

Chapters 8 - 10
1. Why did Dubauwoodnt Kumalo ask Msimangu to walk instead of taking a bus?
   The natives (who used the bus system) were protesting a fare increase and were refusing to ride the bus lines.

2. Why is the government more afraid of Dubula than Tomlinson or John Kumalo?
   Tomlinson has the brains, John has the voice, but Dubula has the heart.

3. What did Mrs. Mkize tell them about Absalom?
   She said he had been there but had left. He had been stealing goods and was in bad company. She thought the taxi driver Hlabeni might know of Absalom's whereabouts.

4. What is the point of Chapter 9 in relationship to the novel's themes?
   Chapter 9 is used to emphasize, elaborate on and personalize the terrible conditions under which the natives of South Africa were living.

5. When Kumalo finally reached Pimville, where Absalom was supposed to be living, what did he find?
   He found a young native girl with whom Absalom was supposed to be living but whom he had apparently abandoned.

Chapters 11 - 14
1. A certain news headline and article grabbed the attention of the priests at the Mission House. What was the article about?
   It was about the murder of a young white man who was an advocate for the native cause.

2. Identify James and Arthur Jarvis.
   Arthur Jarvis was the young white man who was murdered. James Jarvis was his father.

3. "Cry, the beloved country, these things are not yet at an end." What "things"?
   "Cry for the broken tribe, for the law and the custom that is gone. Aye, and cry aloud for the man who is dead, for the woman and children bereaved."

4. "There are voices crying what must be done, a hundred, a thousand voices." Chapter 12 gives several examples of what these "voices" say. What do they say?
   No one can agree on exactly what should be done to fix the problems of South Africa. Some want more police protection. Some say to give the natives a purpose, a useful lace in society. Some say to increase schooling; others want schooling decreased. Some people want to enforce the pass laws. Others want to totally separate whites and natives.

5. What news of Absalom does Mrs. Ndlela give Msimangu?
   She says that the police are looking for him.

6. To what decisions did Kumalo come in Ezenzeleni?
   He turned his thoughts to rebuilding. "After seeing Johannesburg, he would return with a deeper understanding to Ndotsheni." "One could go back knowing better the things one fought against."

7. Where does Kumalo finally meet Absalom? Describe their meeting.
   He meets his son in jail. The meeting is cool at best. Absalom gives short answers or no answers to Kumalo's questions.

8. How does John decide to handle his son's defense?
   He decides that since there is no proof of his son's involvement (except Absalom's word), they will lie and say his son was not there, that Absalom is just seeking revenge for something else.

Chapters 15 - 17
1. What is Father Vincent's gift to Kumalo?
   He finds a lawyer for Absalom, and he promises to try to make the arrangements to have Absalom married to the girl.

2. Why does Father Vincent say sorrow is better than fear?
   "Fear impoverishes always, while sorrow may enrich."

3. In what way was Kumalo cruel to the girl?
   He made her admit she had been with many men and that it was "not right." Then, he asked if she would live with him, should he be willing. She replied that she would and then that she didn't know how to answer. Kumalo knew that she wouldn't know how to answer, and he only asked her to put her on the spot.

4. To what arrangement do Kumalo and the girl finally agree?
   They decided she would marry Absalom (if it could be arranged) and that she would go live with Kumalo and his wife as their daughter-in-law.

5. Describe the content of the conversation between Mrs. Lithebe and the girl.
   Mrs. Lithebe warned the girl not to betray the old man's faith in her--not to continue in her old ways. Also, Mrs. Lithebe wanted to make sure the girl was contented with the change in her lifestyle.

6. Identify Mr. Carmichael.
   Mr. Carmichael is the attorney who agreed to take Absalom's case pro deo.

Chapters 18 - 21
1. Book II begins with the same sentence as Book I did. Compare and contrast the beginning passages of Book I and Book II.
   Book I starts with the same sentence as Book II, but it goes on to tell of the weak and "native" side of the land. Book II stops after the "green" part, leading one to believe Book II will primarily be about Jarvis.

2. Contrast Jarvis' arrival in Johannesburg with Kumalo's.
   Jarvis flew in to the airport and had a private car waiting, unlike Kumalo who took several trains, tried to take a bus, and finally ended up walking.

3. What was ironic about Arthur Jarvis' death?
   Although he was working for the native cause, he was murdered by a native.

4. Why did Arthur Jarvis read about Lincoln?
   Lincoln faced the problem of "freeing" blacks in America to end slavery. From Lincoln, Arthur Jarvis would have learned a lot about the process of freedom.

5. What were Arthur Jarvis' last written words?
   "Allow me a minute."

Chapters 22 - 25
1. Explain the difference between "justice" and "just."
   "Justice" is when the judge executes the laws. "Just" is when the guilty are punished and the innocent are freed.

2. "No second Johannesburg is needed upon the earth. One is enough." Explain why not.
   It is bad enough that one city is so unjust, so full of terrible conditions for the poor and o full of crime. One hopes that there would be no other cities like that.

3. Why was Jarvis "sick at heart" as he read some of his son's papers?
   His son had written "From them [his parents] I learned all that a child should learn of honor and charity and generosity. But of South Africa I learned nothing at all."

4. Why did Kumalo appear to be ill when Jarvis opened the door?
    He wasn't expecting Jarvis at the door, and he felt terrible about his son's actions towards Arthur Jarvis.

5. What was Jarvis' reaction after Kumalo identified himself as the father of his son's murderer?
    At first he was filled with controlled anger, but before Kumalo left, it was obvious that Jarvis did not hold Kumalo responsible. ("Go well, Umfundisi.")

Chapters 26 - 29
1. "There is no applause in prison." Explain the inference regarding John Kumalo.
    John Kumalo has a voice with no heart. He preaches but only for the fame and power. He does not believe enough in his cause to go to prison for it.

2. "Nothing is ever quiet except for fools." Explain.
    Just because there are no outward signs of protest doesn't mean that plans are not being made. Only fools believe that "trouble" is over when protestors are quiet.

3. Why was the headline about another housebreak-murder "bad news"?
    It came just as Absalom's trial was closing, and it would stir up more unrest just as crucial decisions were being made about Absalom's case.

4. What is the verdict for Absalom?
    He was found guilty as charged and sentenced to be hanged.

5. Why did Absalom marry the girl even though he was sentenced to death?
    There was a chance for a pardon for him, although he recognized that the chances of that were slim. Mostly he did it for family pride and to "do the right thing" so his father could provide for the girl and his grandchild.

6. Explain the significance of the name of Peter for Absalom's son.
    It was Peter Jesus called the "rock" upon whom he would build his church. Absalom's child represents the next generation upon which rests the hope for a better future for South Africa.

7. Why did Gertrude leave?
    She realized that she couldn't change enough to do honor to Stephen's home.

Chapters 30 - 32
1. Describe Kumalo's return home.
    He is warmly greeted by friends and family. He introduces the boy and girl to his wife, who welcomes them. He prays. He explains his family situation to a friend whom he expects to tell his friends (and so on) so the villagers will know openly of his family's disgraces.

2. Why did Kumalo visit the chief? What did he want?
   He wanted a school to teach the natives how to care for the land.

3. Who was the small boy who rode to Kumalo's place?
   He was the son of Arthur Jarvis.

4. What is the significance of the boy's trying to learn Zulu?
   Because he is a white boy trying to learn Zulu, it shows that perhaps there is hope for understanding and better communications between the races in the next generation.

5. What was Mr. Jarvis' first gift to the natives of Kumalo's village?
   He sent milk to the children of the village.

Chapters 33 - 36

1. What was Jarvis' second gift to the natives?
   He provided a person to teach them how to care for the land.

2. Who died?
   James Jarvis' wife died.

3. What did Kumalo do for Jarvis? What did the natives do for him?
   Kumalo sent a sympathy note (since a visit would be inappropriate). The natives made a wreath of cypress and white lilies.

4. When the Bishop came for the confirmations, what did he suggest for Kumalo?
   He suggested that Kumalo should be transferred to a place where no one knew of his family's disgraces.

5. Why was Kumalo not transferred?
   A letter to Kumalo came from Jarvis showing his affection for Kumalo and the village and promising to build him a new church. When the Bishop read the letter, he realized that Kumalo should stay.

6. What happened to Absalom?
   He was not pardoned; he was hanged.

7. Why did Kumalo go to the mountain?
   The mountain was his place of spiritual refreshment, his place to be near to God. He went there on the eve of his son's execution.

8. Explain the significance of the fact that the book ends at sunrise.
   Symbolically, sunrise equates to hope--hope for the future of South Africa.

9. The last paragraph of the novel speaks of "the fear of bondage and the bondage of fear." Explain the relevance of this phrase.

> The natives live in fear of bondage (being subservient to whites), and whites live in the bondage of fear (fear of the loss of power and of the natives).

MULTIPLE CHOICE STUDY GUIDE/QUIZ QUESTIONS - *Cry, The Beloved Country*

Chapters 1 - 5

1. What is being described in paragraphs two and three in Chapter 1?
    A. The many industries are being described.
    B. Family life is being described.
    C. Religious beliefs are being described.
    D. The land is being described.

2. True or False: Paragraphs two and three in Chapter 1 deal with one of the central themes of the novel; the deep contrast between the "haves" and the "have nots."
    A. True
    B. False

3. Which of these statements does not describe Reverend Kumalo?
    A. He is the minister of a small church in Ndotsheni.
    B. He is the main character of the novel.
    C. He is the narrator of the story.
    D. He travels to Johannesburg to restore to his family.

4. Who is Reverend Kumalo's brother?
    A. Stephen is his brother.
    B. John is his brother.
    C. Absalom is his brother.
    D. James is his brother.

5. Who is Gertrude?
    A. She is the Reverend's sister.
    B. She is the Reverend's wife.
    C. She is the Reverend's daughter.
    D. She is the Reverend's mother.

6. To what was Reverend Kumalo referring when he said "...once such a thing is opened, it cannot be shut again?"
    A. He was referring to the torment in the soul of a sinner. Once a person faces up to his/her wrong doings, they (the misdeeds) can never again be denied, although they can be forgiven.
    B. He was referring to the digging of the gold mines in South Africa; the land could never be repaired.
    C. He was referring to faith. Once one opens one's heart to faith, it will always be there.
    D. He was referring to a letter he had just received. The reader would be irreversibly affected.

Cry, The Beloved Country Study/Quiz Questions Multiple Choice Page 2

7. One may also symbolically infer that once a person is made aware of a problem, he cannot turn away; the problem will not go away by itself; action must be taken. What is the literary term for this kind of statement?
    A. This is called personification.
    B. This is called foreshadowing.
    C. This is called symbolism.
    D. This is called metaphor.

8. Why did Stephen Kumalo go to Johannesburg?
    A. He went to help his sister who was not well.
    B. He went to attend a religious conference.
    C. He took a temporary job there to earn money to repair his church.
    D. He was thinking of moving there, so he went to see what it was like.

9. True or False: "The lights fall on the grass and stones of a country that sleeps." This quote from the book means that the natives and whites are becoming aware that the problems of social injustice cannot be ignored anymore.
    A. True
    B. False

10. What does "Umfundisi" mean
    A. It means beloved son.
    B. It means a native South African.
    C. It means reverend or pastor.
    D. It means "one who suffers for justice."

11. "The journey had begun and now the fear was back again..." Which of the following was not one of Kumalo's fears?
    A. He had fears of the violence in the city.
    B. He had fears of Gertrude's sickness.
    C. He had fears of getting lost and not being able to find his way home.
    D. He had fears for his son's well-being.

12. What happened to Kumalo when he first arrived in Johannesburg?
    A. A young man pretended to help him but instead stole his money.
    B. He took the wrong train and had to re-trace his route.
    C. He ate some rancid food and got very sick.
    D. He had a panic attack from the stress.

Cry, The Beloved Country Study/Quiz Questions Multiple Choice Page 3

13. Who is Msimangu?
    A. He is a local lawyer who helps newcomers to the city.
    B. He is Kumalo's brother-in-law.
    C. He is a friend of Kumalo's son.
    D. He is a reverend who helps Kumalo.

14. Who is Mrs. Lithebe?
    A. She is the secretary of the local church.
    B. She rents a room to Kumalo.
    C. She is the nurse who has been taking care of Gertrude.
    D. She is a social worker who helps Kumalo.

15. Which of these describes Gertrude's sickness?
    A. She is morally corrupt.
    B. She has multiple personality disorder although no-one realizes it.
    C. She is and has been physically ill for a long time.
    D. She is severely depressed. She has basically given up on life.

16. True or False: Kumalo is very sympathetic to his sister's illness.
    A. True
    B. False

17. What is Kumalo's brother doing in Johannesburg?
    A. He is a doctor in one of the few hospitals that treats natives.
    B. He owns stock in a gold mine.
    C. He is a shop-keeper turned politician. He speaks in public for the natives' cause.
    D. He is also a pastor. Most of his parishioners are natives who have moved to Johannesburg from outlying villages.

18. "The tragedy is not that things are broken. The tragedy is that they are not mended again. What does Msimangu mean?
    A. Life in the villages is becoming more difficult. Many of the young male natives are moving to the cities. The women and elderly who are left can't support the village.
    B. It is bad enough that there is such injustice in South Africa, although one can see how it came about. The wrong comes in that the injustices have not been eliminated since they have been recognized.
    C. The city of Johannesburg is in a state of disrepair. Many of the machines are broken. New buildings cannot be built, an old ones cannot be repaired, because the machinery is not working. The city government is not doing anything to correct the problem.
    D. He is referring to the family problems that Kumalo is having. He is not optimistic that they will be resolved.

Cry, The Beloved Country Study/Quiz Questions Multiple Choice Page 4

19. "It is _____ that rules this land." What rules the land?
    A. The weather rules the land.
    B. God/religion rules the land.
    C. Fear rules the land.
    D. The whites rule the land.

Cry, The Beloved Country Study/Quiz Questions Multiple Choice Page 5

Chapters 6 & 7

20. Which of these does not happen when Kumalo first meets his sister in Johannesburg?
	A. They embrace warmly, happy to see each other.
	B. He asks her each of his questions.
	C. She answers his questions simply and honestly.
	D. She agrees to leave Johannesburg.

21. What did Kumalo do for Gertrude and the child to symbolize starting a new life?
	A. He had them baptized.
	B. He bought them new clothes.
	C. He changed their names.
	D. He held a reception and formally introduced them to his friends.

22. True or False: Kumalo's first meeting with his brother was successful. He confronted his brother, who gave him straightforward answers to his questions.
	A. True
	B. False

23. What is Msimangu's one hope for his country?
	A. He hopes that all of the people will become Christian.
	B. He hopes that more gold will be found, to keep the country prosperous.
	C. He hopes that sickness and poverty will be eradicated in his lifetime.
	D. He hopes that the blacks and whites will work together for the good of their country.

Cry, The Beloved Country Study/Quiz Questions Multiple Choice Page 6

Chapters 8 - 10

24. Why did Dubula ask Kumalo and Msimangu to walk instead of taking a bus?
    A. He wanted them to donate their fare money to a home for orphans.
    B. He knew that a terrorist group was going to attack the bus, and he wanted to save them.
    C. The natives who used the bus were protesting a fare increase and were refusing ride the bus.
    D. He wanted people to use the new free-enterprise taxi system he had started.

25. The government is more afraid of Dubula than of Tomlinson or John Kumalo. What do they say Dubula has?
    A. He has the heart.
    B. He has the brains.
    C. He has the stamina.
    D. He has the voice.

26. What did Mrs. Mkize tell them about Absalom?
    A. He had been stealing goods and was in bad company.
    B. He was attending college and was studying very hard.
    C. He was hiding out in the mountains beyond the city.
    D. He had gone to a pastor in a nearby town to get help for his destructive behavior.

27. What is the point of Chapter 9 in relationship to the novel's themes?
    A. Chapter 9 is used to foreshadow the events to come later in the book.
    B. Chapter 9 is used to compare and contrast the conditions in South Africa before and after the white men came.
    C. Chapter 9 is used to emphasize, elaborate on, and personalize the terrible conditions under which the natives of South Africa were living.
    D. Chapter 9 is used to explain the role of religion in the South African society.

28. When Kumalo finally reached Pimville, where Absalom was supposed to be living, what did he find?
    A. He found Absalom's clothes and belongings but not his son.
    B. He found a young native girl with whom Absalom was supposed to be living but who he had apparently abandoned.
    C. He found a letter from Absalom, saying he was safe, and asking to be left alone.
    D. He found Absalom, sick and discouraged, living in a cardboard shack.

Cry, The Beloved Country Study/Quiz Questions Multiple Choice Page 7

Chapters 11 - 14

29. A certain news headline and article grabbed the attention of the priests at the Mission House. What was the article about?
    A. It was about the murder of a young white man who was an advocate for the native cause.
    B. It was about a riot at one of the mines, led by two young natives.
    C. It was about the terrible conditions in one of the native housing areas, and it was signed "A.K."
    D. It was about the educational inequalities in the native and white schools.

30. Who are James and Arthur Jarvis?
    A. They are two young natives who are trying to organize the others into a politically active group.
    B. They are the owners of the largest gold mines in the area. They are trying to buy out the others, control all of the mines and lower the workers' wages.
    C. They are white friends of John Kumalo.
    D. Arthur Jarvis is a young white man who was an advocate for the native cause, and James Jarvis was his father.

31. "Cry, the beloved country, these things are not yet at an end." Which of the following is not being referred to in this quote from the story?
    A. "...the broken tribe..."
    B. "...the law and custom that is gone..."
    C. "...the decline of family values..."
    D. "...the man who is dead..."

32 - 35 "There are several voices crying what must be done, a hundred, a thousand voices." Chapter 12 gives several examples of what these voices say. Which of the following statements about what the voices say are true, and which are false? (Ch. 12)

32. Some people think more police protection is necessary.
    A. True
    B. False

33. All of the people agree that the natives need to be given a useful place in society.
    A. True
    B. False

34. The natives think the whites should pay higher taxes in order to help the poorer natives.
    A. True
    B. False

Cry, The Beloved Country Study/Quiz Questions Multiple Choice Page 8

35. The Africaans-speaking churches want the restrictions on native labor and enterprise removed.
    A. True
    B. False

36. What news of Absalom does Mrs. Ndlela give Msimangu?
    A. He is safe at a friend's house.
    B. The police are looking for him.
    C. He is on his way back to Ndotsheni.
    D. He is in a reform school.

37. To what decision did Kumalo come in Ezenzeleni?
    A. He would never return to Johannesburg.
    B. He would renounce his ministry.
    C. He would work to rebuild Ndotsheni.
    D. He was too old to do any more; he needed to look for a younger pastor to replace him.

38. Where does Kumalo finally meet Absalom?
    A. They meet in the hospital.
    B. They meet in the lawyer's office.
    C. They meet at Msimangu's church.
    D. They meet at the jail.

39. Which statement describes their meeting?
    A. They are both overcome with emotion.
    B. The meeting is cool at best.

40. How does John decide to handle his son's defense?
    A. He will plea bargain for a lesser sentence by testifying against Absalom.
    B. He will tell the absolute truth and beg for mercy.
    C. He will lie and say that his son wasn't there, that Absalom is seeking revenge for something else.
    D. He will blame the crime on the victim and all whites in general, hoping to generate enough publicity and public sympathy to get the case dismissed.

Cry, The Beloved Country Study/Quiz Questions Multiple Choice Page 9

Chapters 15 - 17

41. True or False: Father Vincent says, "Sorrow impoverishes always, while fear may enrich."
    A. True
    B. False

42. True or False: Father Vincent says, "Sorrow impoverishes always, while fear may enrich."
    A. True
    B. False

43. True or False: Kumalo was very understanding and forgiving to the girl. He didn't ask her any questions.
    A. True
    B. False

44. True or False: Kumalo and the girl agreed that she would marry Absalom and then go to live with Kumalo and his wife as their daughter-in-law.
    A. True
    B. False

45. True or False: Mrs. Lithebe talked to the girl about the advantages of living as a single mother in a large city over living in the country.
    A. True
    B. False

46. True or False: Mr. Carmichael is the attorney who agreed to take Absalom's case pro deo.
    A. True
    B. False

Cry, The Beloved Country Study/Quiz Questions Multiple Choice Page 10

Chapters 18 - 21

47. True or False: Book I and Book II begin with the same sentence.
    A. True
    B. False

48. What is Book II primarily about?
    A. It is primarily about the weak side of the land.
    B. It is primarily about Kumalo's return to Ndotsheni.
    C. It is primarily about Jarvis.
    D. It is primarily about Absalom.

49. True or False: Jarvis and Kumalo used the same means of transportation to get to Johannesburg.
    A. True
    B. False

50. What was ironic about Arthur Jarvis's death?
    A. Although he was working for the native cause, he was murdered by a native.
    B. He was murdered by one of his own servants.
    C. He died on his murderer's birthday.
    D. He was killed with his own gun. One of his servant had stolen it and sold it to a friend, who used it to kill Jarvis.

51. About whom did Arthur Jarvis read to find out about the process of freedom?
    A. He read about George Washington.
    B. He read about Thomas Jefferson.
    C. He read about Abraham Lincoln.
    D. He read about Mohandis Ghandi.

52. What were Arthur Jarvis' last written words?
    A. "There is a lovely road that runs from Ixopo to the hills."
    B. "Here is a chance to try out the experiment of settled mine labour."
    C. "I know what I am fighting for."
    D. "Allow me a minute."

Cry, The Beloved Country Study/Quiz Questions Multiple Choice Page 11

<u>Chapters 22 - 25</u>

53. Which of the following definitions is correct?
    A. "Just" is when the judge executes the laws. "Justice" is when the guilty are punished and the innocent are freed.
    B. "Justice" is when the judge executes the laws. "Just" is when the guilty are punished and the innocent are freed.

54. In Chapter 23, the narrator expresses his opinion about Johannesburg. Which of the following quotes was used?
    A. "Gold, gold, gold. The country is going to be rich again."
    B. "No second Johannesburg is needed upon the earth. One is enough."
    C. "It is hard to be a South African. One can be born an Afrikaner, or an English-speaking South African, or a colored man, or a Zulu."
    D. "I understand better those who have died for their convictions, and have not thought it brave or noble or wonderful to die."

55. What had Arthur Jarvis written that caused his father to become "sick at heart"?
    A. "I am moved by something that is not my own, that moves me to do what is right, at whatever the cost may be."
    B. "I shall do this, not because I am noble or unselfish, but because life slips away, and because I need for the rest of my journey a star that will not play false to me."
    C. "...I learned all that a child should learn of honor and charity and generosity. But of South Africa I learned nothing at all."
    D. " But a man must get something for all his courage and foresight, and there's mental strain, too, to be taken into consideration.

56. Why did Kumalo appear to be ill when Jarvis opened the door
    A. He wasn't expecting Jarvis at the door, and he felt terrible about his son's actions.
    B. He wanted to elicit Jarvis' sympathy.
    C. He really was ill; he had a mild heart attack from the stress of the past few days.
    D. He had never been that close to a white man before, and he panicked.

57. What was Jarvis' reaction after Kumalo identified himself?
    A. He was enraged and attacked Kumalo.
    B. At first he was filled with controlled anger, but then did not hold Kumalo responsible for his son's actions.
    C. He was in such a state of shock that he could not even respond.
    D. He was very sarcastic and condescending, saying that the natives didn't deserve to be helped.

Cry, The Beloved Country Study/Quiz Questions Multiple Choice Page 12

Chapters 26 - 29
All of the questions in this section are True/False

58. True or False: "There is no applause in prison" refers to Absalom. He won't make any friends in prison for killing a white man.
    A. True
    B. False

59. True or False: "Nothing is ever quiet except for fools" means that just because there are no outward signs of protest doesn't mean that plans are not being made. Only fools believe that "trouble" is over when protestors are quiet.
    A. True
    B. False

60. True or False: The headline about another housebreak-murder was bad news because it came just as Absalom's trial was closing.
    A. True
    B. False

61. True or False: Absalom was found guilty, but the judge recommended leniency.
    A. True
    B. False

62. True or False: Absalom married the girl for family pride and to "do the right thing" so his father could provide for the girl and his grandchild.
    A. True
    B. False

63. True or False: Absalom's son was named Peter because Peter was the one who denied Jesus in the garden, just as Absalom had denied his family upbringing by committing his crime.
    A. True
    B. False

64. True or False: Gertrude left because she fell in love with a kind and generous Christian man and married him.
    A. True
    B. False

Cry, The Beloved Country Study/Quiz Questions Multiple Choice Page 13

Chapters 30 -32

65. Which of these does not happen when Kumalo returns home?
    A. He is warmly greeted by his family and friends.
    B. He prays.
    C. He asks a close friend to keep secret all of the information about his problems in Johannesburg.
    D. His wife welcomes the boy and girl.

66. What did Kumalo want from the chief?
    A. He wanted the chief to use his influence to plead for Absalom's life.
    B. He wanted the chief to formally adopt his sister's boy into the tribe.
    C. He wanted to hold a day of mourning for Arthur Jarvis.
    D. He wanted a school to teach the natives how to care for the land.

67. Who was the small boy who rode to Kumalo's place?
    A. He was the chief's son.
    B. He was the son of Arthur Jarvis.
    C. He was no one special; just a little boy out for a ride.
    D. He was the inkosikazi's nephew.

68. How does the author show that there may be hope for better understanding and communication in the next generation?
    A. He shows the boy praying in the small church.
    B. He shows the boy playing with native children.
    C. He shows the boy learning to speak Zulu.
    D. He shows the boy eating dinner in Kumalo's home.

69. What was Mr. Jarvis' first gift to the natives of Kumalo's village?
    A. He gave them milk for their children.
    B. He sent books for the school.
    C. He sent new clothes for everyone.
    D. He had a community telephone installed.

Cry, The Beloved Country Study/Quiz Questions Multiple Choice Page 14

Chapters 33 - 36

70. What was Jarvis' second gift to the natives?
    A. He sent bushels of wheat and corn.
    B. He sent a washing machine for Kumalo's wife.
    C. He sent a person to teach them how to care for the land.
    D. He had a playground build for the children.

71. Which of Jarvis' relatives died?
    A. His grandchild died.
    B. Jarvis' wife died.
    C. His daughter-in-law died.
    D. His mother died.

72. What did Kumalo do?
    A. He sent a sympathy note..
    B. He went to visit and pay his respects.
    C. He held a memorial service in his own church.
    D. He invited Jarvis to spend a day with him.

73. What did the natives do for him?
    A. They collected their best possessions and gave them to Jarvis.
    B. They set up a group of mourners in front of Jarvis' house, as was their custom.
    C. They spent an entire day in silent prayer.
    D. They made a wreath of cypress and white lilies.

74. When the Bishop came for confirmations, what did he suggest for Kumalo?
    A. He suggested that Kumalo should retire.
    B. He suggested that Kumalo should go to confession and beg forgiveness for his failures as the head of the family.
    C. He suggested that Kumalo carry on as if nothing had ever happened.
    D. He suggested that Kumalo be transferred to a place where no one knew of his family's disgrace.

75. What happened to change the Bishop's mind?
    A. The parishioner's staged a protest in favor of Kumalo.
    B. Jarvis sent a complimentary letter and offered to build a new church.
    C. Kumalo's wife begged and pleaded until the Bishop relented.
    D. The Bishop had a dream that Kumalo died of a broken heart. This influenced his final decision because he did not want to be responsible for Kumalo's death.

Cry, The Beloved Country Study/Quiz Questions Multiple Choice Page 15

76. What happened to Absalom?
    A. His cousin helped him escape from the prison. The two were never heard from again.
    B. He killed himself in his cell.
    C. He was hanged.
    D. He received life in prison instead of the death sentence.

77. Where did Kumalo go for spiritual refreshment?
    A. He went to the mountain.
    B. He went into his church.
    C. He went to the river.
    D. He went to the chief's tent.

78. How does the book's ending convey hope for the future of South Africa?
    A. The baby is born.
    B. The rain stops and a rainbow stretches across the sky.
    C. It is sunrise.
    D. Kumalo hugs the little white boy.

79. The last paragraph of the novel speaks of "the fear of bondage and the bondage of fear." Which of the following statements is correct?
    A. The natives live in fear of bondage, and the whites live in the bondage of fear.
    B. The natives live in the bondage of fear, and the whites live in fear of bondage.

ANSWER KEY - MULTIPLE CHOICE STUDY/QUIZ QUESTIONS
Cry, the Beloved Country

Chapters 1-5	Chapters 6-7	Chapters 8-10	Chapters 11-14
1. D	20. A	24. C	29. A
2. A	21. B	25. A	30. D
3. C	22. B	26. A	31. C
4. B	23. D	27. C	32. A
5. A		28. B	33. B
6. D			34. B
7. C			35. B
8. B			36. B
9. A			37. C
10. C			38. D
11. C			39. B
12. A			40. C
13. D			
14. B			
15. A			
16. B			
17. C			
18. B			
19. C			

Chapters 15-17	Chapters 18-21	Chapters 22-29	Chapters 30-36
41. A	47. A	53. B	65. C
42. B	48. C	54. B	66. D
43. B	49. B	55. C	67. B
44. A	50. A	56. A	68. C
45. B	51. C	57. B	69. A
46. A	52. D	58. B	70. C
		59. A	71. B
		60. A	72. A
		61. B	73. D
		62. B	74. D
		63. B	75. B
		64. B	76. C
			77. A
			78. C
			79. A

PREREADING VOCABULARY WORKSHEETS

VOCABULARY - *Cry, The Beloved Country*

<u>Chapters 1-5</u> Part I: Using Prior Knowledge and Contextual Clues
Below are the sentences in which the vocabulary words appear in the text. Read the sentence. Use any clues you can find in the sentence combined with your prior knowledge, and write what you think the underlined words mean in the space provided.

1. They seep into the ground feeding the streams in every <u>kloof</u>.

2. And you can look through the misty panes at green shadowy banks of grass and <u>bracken</u>.

3. And under her eyes the great <u>lorry</u> crushed the life out of her son.

4. My brother, says one, you know the hill that stands so, straight up, behind my father's <u>kraal</u>.

5. In good time no doubt they would come to discuss the reason for this <u>pilgrimage</u> safely at an end.

6. Here in their season grow the blue agapanthus, the wild watsonia, and the red-hot poker, and now and then it happens that one may glimpse an arum in a <u>dell</u>

Part II: Determining the Meaning
Match the vocabulary words to their dictionary definitions. If there are words for which you cannot figure out the definition by contextual clues and by process of elimination, look them up in a dictionary.

____ 1. kloof   A. A motor truck.
____ 2. bracken   B. A small, secluded, wooded valley.
____ 3. lorry   C. Ravine
____ 4. kraal   D. A rural village.
____ 5. pilgrimage   E. A widespread, often weedy fern.
____ 6. dell   F. A long journey or search.

VOCABULARY - Cry The Beloved Country Chapters 6-7

Part I: Using Prior Knowledge and Contextual Clues
    Below are the sentences in which the vocabulary words appear in the text. read the sentence. Use any clues you can find in the sentence combined with your prior knowledge, and write what you think the underlined words mean in the space provided.

1. When he had finished, she burst into a torrent of prayer, of self-<u>denunciation</u>, and urgent petition.

2. You mean, said Msimangu coldly, that she believed in <u>fidelity</u>?

3. Western Native Township which belongs to the <u>Municipality</u> of Johannesburg.

4. She looks at him <u>sullenly</u>, like an animal that is tormented.

5. He smiled his <u>cunning</u> and knowing smile.

6. For there was something in this voice that <u>compelled</u> one to be silent.

7. Now he can <u>gratify</u> his lusts.

8. He stood as though he was testing his <u>exposition</u>.

Part II: Determining the Meaning
    Match the vocabulary words to their dictionary definitions. If there are words for which you cannot figure out the definition by contextual clues and by process of elimination, look them up in a dictionary.

  ___ 1. self-denunciation
  ___ 2. fidelity
  ___ 3. municipality
  ___ 4. sullenly
  ___ 5. cunning
  ___ 6. compelled
  ___ 7. gratify
  ___ 8. exposition

A. A statement or rhetorical discourse intended to give information about or an explanation of difficult material.
B. Showing a brooding ill humor.
C. To please or satisfy.
D. A political unit, such as a city or a town, incorporated for local self-government.
E. A strong, irresistible force; exerted.
F. Self-accusation; self-condemnation.
G. Faithfulness to obligations or duties.
H. Subtlety and deceitful.

VOCABULARY - *Cry The Beloved Country* Chapters 8-10

Part I: Using Prior Knowledge and Contextual Clues

Below are the sentences in which the vocabulary words appear in the text. Read the sentence. Use any clues you can find in the sentence combined with your prior knowledge, and write what you think the underlined words mean in the space provided.

1. At least I had forgotten the boycott of the buses.

2. So getting no peace, she rose irresolute, and went to a room behind.

3. So immersed was he in watching that he was astonished when Msimangu suddenly burst out.

4. I have seen daughters corrupted by boys.

5. Ho, but this man bewilders me.

6. Africa that is my own, delivered in travail from my body, fed from my breast.

7. After all he was a parson, sober and rather dull no doubt.

8. Who indeed knows why there can be comfort in a world of desolation?

9. The little one played endlessly and intently, with a purpose obscure to the adult mind,.

Part II: Determining the Meaning

Match the vocabulary words to their dictionary definitions. If there are words for which you cannot figure out the definition by contextual clues and by process of elimination, look them up in a dictionary.

___ 1. boycott
___ 2. irresolute
___ 3. astonished
___ 4. corrupted
___ 5. bewilders
___ 6. travail
___ 7. parson
___ 8. obscure
___ 9. desolation

A. Barrenness; dreariness; hopelessness
B. Work; painful effort; toil.
C. Hidden; not clearly understood.
D. A member of the clergy, especially a Protestant minister.
E. Unsure of how to act or proceed; undecided.
F. Confuses, befuddles.
G. Marked by immorality and perversion.
H. Filled with sudden wonder or amazement.
I. To abstain from using, buying, or dealing with as a form of protest.

VOCABULARY - *Cry The Beloved Country* Chapters 11-14

Part I: Using Prior Knowledge and Contextual Clues

Below are the sentences in which the vocabulary words appear in the text. Read the sentence. Use any clues you can find in the sentence combined with your prior knowledge, and write what you think the underlined words mean in the space provided.

1. It would seem that a native, probably with two <u>accomplices</u>, entered by the kitchen, thinking no doubt that there would be no one in the house.

2. What lovers can lie sweetly under the stars, when <u>menace</u> grows with the measure of their seclusion?

3-4. So long as we <u>vacillate</u>, so long will we pay dearly for the <u>dubious</u> pleasure of not having to make up our minds.

5. Both European and non-European speakers to present a <u>symposium</u>.

6. Where so many others had gone <u>astray</u> before him.

7. And what did <u>vagabonds</u> do

8. To <u>cleave</u> down between the seeing eyes.

9. And how fools listen to him, silent, <u>enrapt</u>, sighing when he is done, feeding their empty bellies on his empty words.

10. The white <u>warder</u> makes no sign.

Vocabulary *Cry The Beloved Country* Chapters 11-14 Page 2

Part II: Determining the Meaning

Match the vocabulary words to their dictionary definitions. If there are words for which you cannot figure out the definition by contextual clues and by process of elimination, look them up in a dictionary.

___ 1. accomplices
___ 2. menace
___ 3. vacillate
___ 4. dubious
___ 5. symposium

___ 6. Astray
___ 7. vagabonds
___ 8. cleave
___ 9. enrapt
___ 10. warder

A. To fill with rapture or delight.
B. Guard.
C. A meeting or conference for discussion of a topic.
D. To split with a sharp instrument.
E. People without a permanent home who move from place to place
F. A possible danger; a threat.
G. Away from the correct path or direction.
H. Those who aid a lawbreaker in a criminal act.
I. Doubtful.
J. To swing indecisively from one course of action or opinion to another.

VOCABULARY - *Cry The Beloved Country* Chapters 15-17

Part I: Using Prior Knowledge and Contextual Clues

Below are the sentences in which the vocabulary words appear in the text. Read the sentence. Use any clues you can find in the sentence combined with your prior knowledge, and write what you think the underlined words mean in the space provided.

1. Waiting till he could <u>summon</u> strength enough to go to the Mission House.

2. And the way in which he said, that comforted me, was to Father Vincent so <u>unendurable</u>, so he sat there rigid.

3. "Sorrow is better than fear," said Father Vincent <u>doggedly</u>.

4. Kumalo looked at him, not bitterly or accusingly or <u>reproachfully</u>.

5. Yet I cannot see how such a life can be <u>amended</u>.

6. He had seen that this could <u>irritate</u> those who were with him.

7. If you should ever <u>repent</u> of this plan...you must not shut it up inside you, or run away as you did from your mother.

8. His face has fallen into a <u>mould</u> of suffering.

9. She spread out her hands, seeking some gesture to <u>convey</u> her conviction.

Part II: Determining the Meaning

Match the vocabulary words to their dictionary definitions. If there are words for which you cannot figure out the definition by contextual clues and by process of elimination, look them up in a dictionary.

___ 1. summon
___ 2. unendurable
___ 3. doggedly
___ 4. reproachfully
___ 5. amended
___ 6. irritate
___ 7. repent
___ 8. mould
___ 9. convey

A. To feel such regret for past conduct as to change one's mind regarding it.
B. Expressing blame.
C. General shape or form.
D. Annoy, bother.
E. Gather together.
F. To communicate or make known.
G. Improved.
H. Stubbornly persevering; tenaciously.
I. Unbearable.

VOCABULARY - *Cry The Beloved Country* Chapters 18-21

Part I: Using Prior Knowledge and Contextual Clues

Below are the sentences in which the vocabulary words appear in the text. Read the sentence. Use any clues you can find in the sentence combined with your prior knowledge, and write what you think the underlined words mean in the space provided.

1. When they visited one another and sat on the long cool <u>verandahs</u> drinking their tea, they must needs look out over the barren valleys.

2. But a boy with education did not want to work on the farms, and went off to the towns to look for more <u>congenial</u> occupation.

3. He rang <u>viciously</u>, and got no answer.

4. We arranged the funeral <u>provisionally</u> for tomorrow afternoon.

5. It's a <u>lingo</u> I know nothing about, thank God.

6. She lay there thinking of it, the pain was deep, deep and <u>ineluctable</u>.

7. I am <u>compelled</u> by the Annual Meeting to congratulate you with this matter.

8. It was <u>permissible</u> to develop our great resources with the aid of what labour we could find.

9. Such development has only one true name, and that is <u>exploitation</u>.

10. It was permissible to believe that its destruction was <u>inevitable</u>.

11. There wouldn't be any <u>subsidies</u>.

Vocabulary - *Cry The Beloved Country* Chapters 18-21 Page 2

Part II: Determining the Meaning

Match the vocabulary words to their dictionary definitions. If there are words for which you cannot figure out the definition by contextual clues and by process of elimination, look them up in a dictionary.

___ 1. verandahs
___ 2. congenial
___ 3. viciously
___ 4. provisionally
___ 5. lingo
___ 6. ineluctable
___ 7. compelled
___ 8. permissible
___ 9. exploitation
___ 10. inevitable
___ 11. subsidies

A. Suited to one's needs or nature; agreeable.
B. Monetary assistance granted by a government.
C. Impossible to avoid or prevent.
D. Taking advantage of people or a situation for monetary gain.
E. Permitted; allowable
F. Language.
G. Temporarily.
H. Forced to action.
I. Aggressively; savagely.
J. A porch or balcony, usually roofed and often partly enclosed, extending along the outside of a building.
K. Not to be avoided or escaped; inevitable.

VOCABULARY - *Cry The Beloved Country* Chapters 22-29

Part I: Using Prior Knowledge and Contextual Clues
　　Below are the sentences in which the vocabulary words appear in the text. Read the sentence. Use any clues you can find in the sentence combined with your prior knowledge, and write what you think the underlined words mean in the space provided.

1. At the back of the Court there are seats rising in tiers.

2. Therefore a Judge must be incorruptible.

3. Says that Absalom Kumalo will plead guilty to culpable homicide, but not to murder for he had no intention to kill.

4. I shall do this, not because I am a negrophile and a hater of my own , but because I cannot find it in me to do anything else.

5. I have married a wife who thinks as I do, who has tried to conquer her own fears and hates; aspiration is thus made easy.

6. Jarvis picked it up and restored it to him, but the old man put it down as a hindrance.

7. They stood looking at each other without words, bound in a great constraint.

Part II: Determining the Meaning
　　Match the vocabulary words to their dictionary definitions. If there are words for which you cannot figure out the definition by contextual clues and by process of elimination, look them up in a dictionary.

　　___ 1. tiers
　　___ 2. incorruptible
　　___ 3. culpable
　　___ 4. negrophile
　　___ 5. aspiration
　　___ 6. hindrance
　　___ 7. constraint

A. Awkwardness.
B. A strong desire for high achievement; ambition.
C. Deserving of blame or censure as being wrong.
D. An impediment; something that gets in the way.
E. Incapable of being swayed to do anything immoral, illegal or unethical.
F. One of a series of rows placed one above another.
G. One friendly to Negroes and their interests.

VOCABULARY - *Cry The Beloved Country* Chapters 30-36

Part I: Using Prior Knowledge and Contextual Clues

Below are the sentences in which the vocabulary words appear in the text. Read the sentence. Use any clues you can find in the sentence combined with your prior knowledge, and write what you think the underlined words mean in the space provided.

1. The boys are calling and crying, with the queer <u>tremulous</u> call that is known in this country.

2. The love of God, and the fellowship of the Holy Spirit be with you and <u>abide</u> with you.

3. For this is a <u>prelude</u>, it is only a beginning.

4. He sat frowning and <u>perplexed</u>.

5. The headmaster was polite and <u>obliging</u> behind the great spectacles.

6. Or was his vision a <u>delusion</u>?

7. Kumalo shook himself out of his <u>reverie</u>.

8. While there was quite an <u>array</u> of sticks and flags, and Kumalo looked on as mystified as ever.

9. They knew that the storm was <u>abating</u>.

10. But there came a picture to him of the house of <u>bereavement</u>.

11. Oh, the grave and the <u>sombre</u> words.

VOCABULARY - *Cry The Beloved Country* Chapters 30-36 Page 2

Part II: Determining the Meaning
   Match the vocabulary words to their dictionary definitions. If there are words for which you cannot figure out the definition by contextual clues and by process of elimination, look them up in a dictionary.

___ 1. tremulous
___ 2. abide
___ 3. prelude
___ 4. perplexed
___ 5. obliging
___ 6. delusion
___ 7. reverie
___ 8. array
___ 9. abating
___ 10. bereavement
___ 11. sombre

A. Willing to do a service or favor for.
B. Grief over someone's death.
C. Daydream.
D. Display.
E. A false belief or opinion.
F. Dark; gloomy; serious; grave.
G. Introduction.
H. To remain in a place.
I. Lessening.
J. Marked by trembling, quivering, or shaking.
K. Confused or troubled with uncertainty or doubt.

VOCABULARY ANSWER KEY - *Cry, The Beloved Country*

Chapters 1-5
1. C
2. E
3. A
4. D
5. F
6. B

Chapters 6-7
1. F
2. G
3. D
4. B
5. H
6. E
7. C
8. A

Chapters 8-10
1. I
2. E
3. H
4. G
5. F
6. B
7. D
8. C
9. A

Chapters 11-14
1. H
2. F
3. J
4. I
5. C
6. G
7. E
8. D
9. A
10. B

Chapters 15-17
1. E
2. I
3. H
4. B
5. G
6. D
7. A
8. C
9. F

Chapters 18-21
1. J
2. A
3. I
4. G
5. F
6. K
7. H
8. E
9. D
10. C
11. B

Chapters 22-29
1. F
2. E
3. C
4. G
5. B
6. D
7. A

Chapters 30-36
1. J
2. H
3. G
4. K
5. A
6. E
7. C
8. D
9. I
10. B
11. F

DAILY LESSONS

LESSON ONE

Objectives
1. To introduce the *Cry, the Beloved Country* unit.
2. To distribute books and other related materials
3. To preview the study questions for chapters 1-5
4. To familiarize students with the vocabulary for chapters 1-5

Activity #1
Distribute the materials students will use in this unit. Explain in detail how students are to use these materials.

Study Guides Students should read the study guide questions for each reading assignment prior to beginning the reading assignment to get a feeling for what events and ideas are important in the section they are about to read. After reading the section, students will (as a class or individually) answer the questions to review the important events and ideas from that section of the book. Students should keep the study guides as study materials for the unit test.

Vocabulary Prior to reading a reading assignment, students will do vocabulary work related to the section of the book they are about to read. Following the completion of the reading of the book, there will be a vocabulary review of all the words used in the vocabulary assignments. Students should keep their vocabulary work as study materials for the unit test.

Reading Assignment Sheet You need to fill in the reading assignment sheet to let students know by when their reading has to be completed. You can either write the assignment sheet up on a side blackboard or bulletin board and leave it there for students to see each day or you can "ditto" copies for each student to have. In either case, you should advise students to become very familiar with the reading assignments so they know what is expected of them.

Extra Activities Center The Extra Activities page of this unit contains suggestions for an extra library of related books and articles in your classroom as well as crossword and word search puzzles. Make an extra activities center in your room where you will keep these materials for students to use. (Bring the books and articles in from the library and keep several copies of the puzzles on hand.) Explain to students that these materials are available for students to use when they finish reading assignments or other class work early.

Nonfiction Assignment Sheet Explain to students that they each are to read at least one non-fiction piece from the in-class library at some time during the unit. Students will fill out a nonfiction assignment sheet after completing the reading to help you evaluate their reading experiences and to help the students think about and evaluate their own reading experiences. Students may use the information they read for the introductory research project to fulfill their nonfiction reading assignment for this unit.

Books Each school has its own rules and regulations regarding student use of school books. Advise students of the procedures that are normal for your school.

Activity #3
Tell students that prior to your next class period they should have previewed the study questions and done the prereading vocabulary worksheet for Chapters 1-5. Students should also have read Chapters 1-5 of *Cry, the Beloved Country*.

NONFICTION ASSIGNMENT SHEET
(To be completed after reading the required nonfiction article)

Name _____ Date _____

Title of Nonfiction Read _____

Written By _____ Publication Date _____

I. Factual Summary: Write a short summary of the piece you read.

II. Vocabulary
    1. With which vocabulary words in the piece did you encounter some degree of difficulty?

    2. How did you resolve your lack of understanding with these words?

III. Interpretation: What was the main point the author wanted you to get from reading his work?

IV. Criticism
    1. With which points of the piece did you agree or find easy to accept? Why?

    2. With which points of the piece did you disagree or find difficult to believe? Why?

V. Personal Response: What do you think about this piece? <u>OR</u> How does this piece influence your ideas?

LESSON TWO

Objectives
1. To review the main ideas and events from chapters 1-5
2. To introduce students to the background research project for this unit
3. To give students the opportunity to find and read information for the research project

Activity #1
Give students a few minutes to formulate answers for the study guide questions for chapters 1-5, and then discuss the answers to the questions in detail. Write the answers on the board or overhead transparency so students can have the correct answers for study purposes.

NOTE: It is a good practice in public speaking and leadership skills for individual students to take charge of leading the discussions of the study questions. Perhaps a different student could go to the front of the class and lead the discussion each day that the study questions are discussed during this unit. Of course, the teacher should guide the discussion when appropriate and be sure to fill in any gaps the students leave.

Activity #2
Distribute the Project Assignment Sheet. Discuss the directions in detail. Take your class to your school's library/media center so they can begin working on the project.

LESSON THREE

Objectives
1. To evaluate students' research
2. To prepare students for their oral reports
3. To give students the opportunity to practice writing to inform
4. To give the teacher the opportunity to evaluate students' writing skills

Activity #1
Distribute Writing Assignment #1. Discuss the directions in detail. Give students ample time to complete the assignment.

Activity #2
Tell students that prior to your next class meeting they should have done the prereading and reading work for chapters 6-7.

RESEARCH PROJECT ASSIGNMENT SHEET - *Cry, the Beloved Country*

PROMPT

You can read *Cry, the Beloved Country* as a book unto itself without knowing anything else about South Africa. However, the book will be much more meaningful for you if you learn a little bit about South Africa, too.

The purpose of this assignment is to give you the opportunity to learn more about South Africa so you can not only better appreciate the book *Cry, the Beloved Country*, but also so you can better understand the place of South Africa in our world today and our relationship with that country.

ASSIGNMENT

Each of you must read at least two articles about South Africa. You may use magazine articles, articles from encyclopedias, chapters in books, travel brochures, or any printed matter you can find about that country.

You will have the remainder of this class time to find and begin to read your articles. In our next class meeting, you will write a written report about your articles in preparation for an oral report in the following class period(s).

GETTING STARTED

There are hundreds of topics related to South Africa. South Africa has an interesting mixture of people, which, in turn, makes for an interesting political scene. It has enormous natural resources and a variety of topographical features. In the past ten years South Africa has been in the news frequently--primarily for issues relating to "apartheid," the Afrikaan word for social segregation. You should be able to easily find a wealth of information about the country and people of South Africa.

SKIM OVER THE ARTICLES. GO BACK AND THOROUGHLY READ THEM. SKIM THROUGH THEM AGAIN, AND THIS TIME JOT DOWN NOTES ABOUT THE MAIN IDEAS THAT ARE PRESENTED. YOU WILL NEED THESE NOTES FOR YOUR PRESENTATION.

THE PRESENTATION

You will be required to make an oral presentation about the articles you read. The presentation does not have to be long, but you do have to let the rest of us know the most important points you found in your reading. Most presentations will probably last 2-5 minutes.

WRITING ASSIGNMENT #1 - *Cry, the Beloved Country*

PROMPT
You have read at least two articles about South Africa. Now write a composition in which you tell about the articles you read. Think of this as a script for your oral presentation. By doing this writing assignment, you will gather and organize your facts thus preparing yourself for your oral presentation.

PREWRITING
You have done most of your prewriting work already by taking notes as you read your articles. If you took notes in order from the beginning of the article to the end of the article, your notes will have a natural flow to them and will probably need little organizing. If you took notes in a haphazard fashion, you will need to organize them so that the ideas flow naturally, one to another.

DRAFTING
The easiest way to write this composition is to write an introductory paragraph in which you introduce the topics your articles were about. Then, take your articles one at a time. Write one paragraph (or more if necessary) telling the facts of your first article. Write a paragraph (or more if necessary) telling the facts of your second article. Write a paragraph in which you give your own response to the information you collected.

PROMPT
When you finish the rough draft of your paper, ask a student who sits near you to read it. After reading your rough draft, he/she should tell you what he/she liked best about your work, which parts were difficult to understand, and ways in which your work could be improved. Reread your paper considering your critic's comments and make the corrections you think are necessary.

PROOFREADING
Do a final proofreading of your paper double-checking your grammar, spelling, organization, and the clarity of your ideas.

LESSON FOUR

Objectives
1. To review the main ideas and events of chapters 6-7
2. To preview and read chapters 8-10
3. To expose all students to a variety of information about South Africa
4. To give students the opportunity to practice public speaking

Activity #1
Give students a few minutes to formulate answers for the study guide questions for chapters 6-7 and then discuss the answers to the questions in detail. Write the answers on the board or overhead transparency so students can have the correct answers for study purposes.

Activity #2
Tell students that prior to Lesson Six (give students a day/date), they should have done the prereading and reading work for chapters 8-10.

Activity #3
Ask each student to give a brief oral report about the nonfiction work he/she read for the research project assignment. Your criteria for evaluating this report will vary depending on the level of your students. You may wish for students to give a complete report without using notes of any kind, or you may want students to read directly from a written report, or you may want to do something in between these two extremes. Just make students aware of your criteria in ample time for them to prepare their reports.

Start with one student's report. After that, ask if anyone else in the class has read about a topic related to the first student's report. If no one has, choose another student at random. After each report, be sure to ask if anyone has a report related to the one just completed. That will help keep a continuity during the discussion of the reports.

LESSON FIVE

Objectives
1. To expose all students to a wealth of information about South Africa
2. To give students the opportunity to practice their public speaking skills

Activity
Continue the oral presentations begun in Lesson Four as described there.

LESSON SIX

Objectives
1. To review the main ideas and events of chapters 8-10
2. To conclude the oral reports
3. To preview and read chapters 11-14

Activity #1
   Give students a few minutes to formulate answers for the study guide questions for chapters 8-10 and then discuss the answers to the questions in detail. Write the answers on the board or overhead transparency so students can have the correct answers for study purposes.

Activity #2
   Tell students that prior to your next class meeting they should have done the prereading and reading work for chapters 11-14. If time remains in this class period after the oral presentations have concluded, students may work on this assignment.

Activity #3
   Continue and conclude the oral reports about South Africa.

LESSON SEVEN

Objectives
1. To review the main ideas and events from chapters 11-14
2. To preview and read chapters 15-17
3. To evaluate students' oral reading skills

Activity # 1
   Give students a few minutes to formulate answers for the study guide questions for chapters 11-14 and then discuss the answers to the questions in detail. Write the answers on the board or overhead transparency so students can have the correct answers for study purposes.

Activity #2
   Give students about ten to fifteen minutes to preview the study questions and do the prereading vocabulary work for chapters 15-17.

Activity #3
   Have students read chapters 15-17 of *Cry, the Beloved Country* out loud in class. If you have not yet completed an oral reading evaluation for your students this marking period, this would be a good opportunity to do so. A form is included with this unit for your convenience.

ORAL READING EVALUATION - *Cry, the Beloved Country*

Name _____ Class _____ Date _____

SKILL	EXCELLENT	GOOD	AVERAGE	FAIR	POOR
Fluency	5	4	3	2	1
Clarity	5	4	3	2	1
Audibility	5	4	3	2	1
Pronunciation	5	4	3	2	1
_____	5	4	3	2	1
_____	5	4	3	2	1

Total _____   Grade _____

Comments:

LESSON EIGHT

Objectives
1. To review the main ideas and events for chapters 15-17
2. To preview and read chapters 18-21
3. To get students to think about the extra material that was presented
4. To give students the opportunity to express their personal opinions
5. To give the teacher the opportunity to evaluate students' writing skills
6. To help prepare students for the second project that goes along with this unit

Activity #1
Give students a few minutes to formulate answers for the study guide questions for chapters 15-17 and then discuss the answers to the questions in detail. Write the answers on the board or overhead transparency so students can have the correct answers for study purposes.

Activity #2
Tell students that prior to your next class meeting they should have completed the prereading and reading work for chapters 18-21. If they finish the writing assignment early, they may begin this reading assignment.

Activity #3
Distribute Writing Assignment #2. Discuss the directions in detail and give students ample time to complete the assignment.

LESSON NINE

Objectives
1. To review the main ideas and events of chapters 18-21
2. To preview and read chapters 22-29
3. To evaluate students' oral reading skills

Activity #1
Give students a few minutes to formulate answers for the study guide questions for chapters 18-21 and then discuss the answers to the questions in detail. Write the answers on the board or overhead transparency so students can have the correct answers for study purposes.

Activity #2
Give students about fifteen minutes to preview the study questions and do the vocabulary work for chapters 22-29. Have students read chapters 22-29 orally in class. Continue the oral reading evaluations. Tell students that this assignment must be completed prior to your next class meeting.

WRITING ASSIGNMENT #2 - *Cry, the Beloved Country*

PROMPT
You have heard and read a great many facts relating to South Africa, and you have had some time to think about those facts. Now you are to turn into a roving reporter, getting opinions from others about the information you have all heard.

Your assignment is to write down five questions. The questions must prompt the person you are asking to give a personal opinion about the information reported in class about South Africa. Each question should focus on a different aspect of the information presented.

After you write down your questions, interview three of your classmates (separately), ask each of the three classmates all five questions and write down their responses.

PREWRITING
Most of your prewriting has been done through your reading and the oral reports; you have information about which to ask questions. Review your notes from the oral reports. Make a list of topics that were covered in the reports. Think about each topic. Brainstorm a list of questions related to those topics.

Look through your list of topics and decide which ones will provoke an opinion as an answer. Put a star next to those questions. Which of the starred questions will prompt the most interesting responses from the people you interview? Circle those questions. Choose five of the circled questions to use for your interviews. Your questions must require more than "Yes" or "No" answers.

Find a classmate who is available to be interviewed. Ask him/her your five questions and write down his/her answers. When you finish with one interview, go to another student and do another interview. Interview a total of three classmates and then review your notes prior to drafting.

DRAFTING
Put your usual heading at the top of your paper. Write down the first question you asked. Under that, write the responses from each of the three people you interviewed. Write one good paragraph for each response. Label each response: "Response 1," "Response 2," and "Response 3." Repeat this pattern for each of the questions you asked and responses you received.

PROMPT
When you finish the rough draft of your composition, ask a student who sits near you to read it. After reading your rough draft, he/she should tell you what he/she liked best about your work, which parts were difficult to understand, and ways in which your work could be improved. Reread your paper considering your critic's comments and make the corrections you think are necessary. Do a final proofreading of your paper double-checking your grammar, spelling, organization, and the clarity of your ideas.

LESSON ELEVEN

Objectives
1. To review the main ideas and events from chapters 30-36
2. To discuss *Cry, the Beloved Country* on interpretive and critical levels

Activity #1
Take a few minutes at the beginning of the period to review the study questions for chapters 30-36.

Activity #2
Choose the questions from the Extra Discussion Questions/Writing Assignments which seem most appropriate for your students. A class discussion of these questions is most effective if students have been given the opportunity to formulate answers to the questions prior to the discussion. To this end, you may either have all the students formulate answers to all the questions, divide your class into groups and assign one or more questions to each group, or you could assign one question to each student in your class. The option you choose will make a difference in the amount of class time needed for this activity.

Activity #3
After students have had ample time to formulate answers to the questions, begin your class discussion of the questions and the ideas presented by the questions. Be sure students take notes during the discussion so they have information to study for the unit test.

EXTRA WRITING ASSIGNMENTS/DISCUSSION QUESTIONS - *Cry, the Beloved Country*

Interpretation

1. From what point of view is *Cry, the Beloved Country* written? What advantages did using that point of view give the author?

2. If you were to rewrite *Cry, the Beloved Country* as a play, where would you start and end each act? Explain why.

3. Where is the climax of the story. Explain your choice.

4. What are the main conflicts in the novel? Are they all resolved? If so, how? If not, why not?

Critical

6. Why was Absalom hanged and not pardoned? (Paton could have written it either way.) What effect would a pardon have had on the themes of the novel?

7. Are Kumalo's actions believably motivated? Explain why or why not.

8. Explain the importance of the setting in *Cry, the Beloved Country*. Could this story have been set in a different time and place and still have the same effect?

9. Characterize Alan Paton's style of writing. How does it contribute to the value of the novel?

10. Discuss the validity of using the city as a "bad" place and the country as a "good" place.

11. Explain how the title relates to the events of the novel and the themes of *Cry, the Beloved Country*.

12. Find examples of Paton's use of irony in *Cry, the Beloved Country* and discuss their effect on the novel.

16. Are the characters in *Cry, the Beloved Country* stereotypes? If so, explain why Alan Paton used stereotypes. If not, explain how the characters merit individuality.

17. In what ways did Stephen Kumalo come back to his village a wiser man for having taken his trip to Johannesburg?

18. Stephen Kumalo's age is often stressed in the novel, as is the youth of the girl, Gertrude's son, and the unborn child. Explain why.

Cry, the Beloved Country Extra Discussion Questions page 2

Personal Response

17. How would you propose to solve South Africa's racial injustices?

18. Who is responsible for Absalom's death?

19. Did you enjoy reading *Cry, the Beloved Country*? Why or why not?

20. Compare and contrast racial injustices in South Africa with racial injustices in America.

21. Compare and contrast the reasons for homelessness in *Cry, the Beloved Country* with the reasons for homelessness in the United States today.

22. If you were to go to Johannesburg today, what would life in the city be like compared to the way it is portrayed in the book?

LESSON TWELVE

Objective
　　To review all of the vocabulary work done in this unit

Activity
　　Choose one (or more) of the vocabulary review activities listed below and spend your class period as directed in the activity. Some of the materials for these review activities are located in the Extra Activities section of this unit.

VOCABULARY REVIEW ACTIVITIES

1. Divide your class into two teams and have an old-fashioned spelling or definition bee.

2. Give each of your students (or students in groups of two, three or four) a *Cry, the Beloved Country* Vocabulary Word Search Puzzle. The person (group) to find all of the vocabulary words in the puzzle first wins.

3. Give students a *Cry, the Beloved Country* Vocabulary Word Search Puzzle without the word list. The person or group to find the most vocabulary words in the puzzle wins.

4. Use a *Cry, the Beloved Country* Vocabulary Crossword Puzzle. Put the puzzle onto a transparency on the overhead projector (so everyone can see it), and do the puzzle together as a class.

5. Give students a *Cry, the Beloved Country* Vocabulary Matching Worksheet to do.

6. Divide your class into two teams. Use the *Cry, the Beloved Country* vocabulary words with their letters jumbled as a word list. Student 1 from Team A faces off against Student 1 from Team B. You write the first jumbled word on the board. The first student (1A or 1B) to unscramble the word wins the chance for his/her team to score points. If 1A wins the jumble, go to student 2A and give him/her a definition. He/she must give you the correct spelling of the vocabulary word which fits that definition. If he/she does, Team A scores a point, and you give student 3A a definition for which you expect a correctly spelled matching vocabulary word. Continue giving Team A definitions until some team member makes an incorrect response. An incorrect response sends the game back to the jumbled-word face off, this time with students 2A and 2B. Instead of repeating giving definitions to the first few students of each team, continue with the student after the one who gave the last incorrect response on the team. For example, if Team B wins the jumbled-word face-off, and student 5B gave the last incorrect answer for Team B, you would start this round of definition questions with student 6B, and so on. The team with the most points wins!

7. Have students write a story in which they correctly use as many vocabulary words as possible. Have students read their compositions orally! Post the most original compositions on your bulletin board.

LESSON THIRTEEN

Objectives
1. To give students the opportunity to practice writing to persuade
2. To give the teacher the opportunity to evaluate students' writing skills
3. To have students prepare materials that will be used in the unit project

Activity
Distribute Writing Assignment #3. Discuss the directions in detail and give students ample time to complete the assignment.
While students are working on this assignment, call individual students to your desk or some other private area for a writing conference based on the first two writing assignments in this unit. An evaluation form is provided to help structure your conferences.

LESSONS FOURTEEN - SEVENTEEN

Objectives
1. To bring together all the elements students have been studying in this unit
2. To review the ideas in the unit
3. To give students practical experience in organizing and presenting information
4. To give students practice comparing, contrasting and evaluating information

Activity #1
Distribute the Unit Project Assignment and discuss the directions in detail.

TEACHER NOTES:
The length of time this project takes will depend on the level of your students and how involved you decide you want to get.
This unit plan is based on using Lesson Fourteen as a planning session in which students decide what types of things and what format they wish to use in their video. Lesson Fifteen would be used for students to write scripts and compile the appropriate materials. Lesson Sixteen would be a working session to finalize the scripts, rehearse and/or begin filming. Lesson Seventeen would be for filming, and Lesson Eighteen would be for viewing the film.
You might want to decide what students will put in the film (or what structure they will use) if you have a lower level class. Middle and upper level classes should be able to devise their own format. This unit assumes you have a middle or upper level class.
The earlier part of this unit was designed to create ample materials for students to use and edit for this video. Students have piles of factual information from research and Writing Assignment #1. They have opinions about all of those topics from Writing Assignment #2 with which they might have a "man on the street" interview section on the video. Finally, Writing Assignment #3 provides students with the material for short, educational "commercials" between their stories, interviews, etc. Encourage the use of visual aids, graphics, pictures, costumes, props, etc.

WRITING ASSIGNMENT #3 - *Cry, the Beloved Country*

PROMPT

Every day you are bombarded with a sea of persuasive arguments ranging from parents trying to get you out of bed and off to school ("I've told you three times to get up and get ready for school; now get up or else . . . ."), to teachers trying to get you to pay attention and do your work ("Pay attention! There will be a quiz next week, and you had better know this information!"), to coaches persuading you to give your best efforts at practice ("You guys had better shape up and put forth some effort if you hope to beat _____ on Friday night!), to businesses trying to get you and your parents to buy their products (Commercials on television and radio are great examples of persuasive arguments.).

There are other more subtle forms of persuasion--a look from a friend that says, "If you don't do this, you're definitely not cool," a slanted news story that gives only one side of the story making that side appear to be right, a little comment here or there that helps to form your opinions about an issue, a person, or an idea, and so on. Many times we don't even recognize the fact that we are being manipulated (That's what persuasion is--manipulation!).

You can never practice the art of persuasion too much. It's like practicing magic or a card trick. You can learn to do it so well that the person or people you are persuading will never know they are being persuaded, just like the audience never knows how the magician did the trick. Why? Why would you want to have this skill? Think about it. Imagine always getting your own way, having people do what you want them to do without much of an argument. You've heard of "the art of persuasion"; there is another saying: "the power of persuasion." If you are good at the art of persuasion, you have power.

Your assignment is to write a script for a television commercial (30 seconds long) relating to South Africa. For example, you could do a commercial against apartheid or a commercial enticing tourists to come to South Africa. Other topics could be to protect the endangered species found in South Africa or to purchase some item that is made in South Africa. Think of a South African topic that interests you; you don't have to use one of these ideas.

PREWRITING

Choose a topic about which you want to do your commercial. Answer these questions: What is the purpose of the commercial? Who is the audience? Of what am I going to persuade the audience? What is most likely to persuade them? Make a list of the things that would be likely to persuade your audience. Circle your best ideas. Jot down notes about how each could be incorporated into your commercial. If something won't fit in, decide whether or not it is important enough to devise a way to keep it in, or if it would be just as well left out. Make a little outline description of your commercial.

Writing Assignment #3 *Cry, the Beloved Country* Page 2

DRAFTING

Under the heading PURPOSE, state the purpose of your commercial. Under the heading MATERIALS, make a list of props/materials needed to create the commercial. Under the heading ACTION, describe your commercial as you see the finished product. Under the heading MISCELLANEOUS, put in any notes, comments, or directions--or anything that you feel is important to mention but won't fit in the other headings.

PROOFREADING

When you finish the rough draft of your commercial, ask a student who sits near you to read it. After reading your rough draft, he/she should tell you what he/she liked best about your work, which parts were difficult to understand, and ways in which your work could be improved. Reread your paper considering your critic's comments and make the corrections you think are necessary.

Do a final proofreading of your paper double-checking your grammar, spelling, organization, and the clarity of your ideas.

WRITING EVALUATION FORM - *Cry, the Beloved Country*

Name _____ Date _____

Grammar: correct   errors noted on paper

Spelling: correct   errors noted on paper

Punctuation: correct   errors noted on paper

Legibility: excellent   good   fair   poor

Strengths:

Weaknesses:

Comments/Suggestions:

UNIT PROJECT ASSIGNMENT - *Cry, the Beloved Country*

PROMPT

You have done a great deal of work in this unit finding out about South Africa, and you have accumulated considerable knowledge on the topic. It's time to share the wealth. Other classes of students in history or social studies, for example, often study South Africa. (Who knows? Perhaps such a study in another class is in *your* future!) Given a choice between going to the library and digging out the information as you have done, or watching a great video that tells you everything you would need to know, which would you choose? . . . . Thought so! So you are going to create a video that includes everything a person needs to know about South Africa.

REQUIREMENTS

* The video must last between 40 and 50 minutes.
* It must include basic facts about South Africa
   (location, topography, climate, population, culture, natural resources, etc.).
* It must include some history of South Africa.
* It must include current issues in South Africa.
* Everyone in the class must contribute to the video.

GETTING STARTED

1. **Decide on a basic format.**
   What kind of a video would you like to watch? A video with someone like Dan Rather sitting at a desk reading off facts or a teacher standing in the front of the room lecturing? Or would you prefer to watch a video that has humor, action, music, and presents the material in an interesting way? Detail what kinds of ideas pop into your head and make a list.

2. **Decide on what categories of information must be covered in the video.**
   Make a list of the categories of information that need to be included. Next to each category, make a little list of ideas about how that information could be presented.

3. **Consider the information you already have created and gathered** through the three writing assignments in this unit.
   Make notes about ways you could use the materials and facts you have already created. You have basic facts, opinions, and persuasive commercials already composed on a variety of topics.

4. **Combine and summarize your thoughts from 1-3 above.**
   Come to definite decisions about what should be in the video and how it should be presented. Make a list of things that will be included, and next to the items, make notes about how they will be presented. Assign each item an amount of time in which it must be presented in the video. The most important items should have the most time, and the least important items should have the least time.

Cry, the Beloved Country Project Assignment Continued

5. **Make a list of things that need to be done.**
   Start with the first item on your list from 4. above. Make a list of specific tasks that must be done to get ready for filming this segment. Make a list of props needed, if any. Do this for each item on the list and then assign one person to do each task. (A task may be writing a script, making a map, creating a costume, or anything that needs to be done.) Read the list of props needed, and see who can bring items to class. Decide where and how to make or get the items no one in class has readily available.

6. **Do the tasks.**
   Make sure everyone knows what needs to be done, what he/she is expected to do, and by when each task must be completed.

7. **Rehearse.**

8. **Film.**

LESSON NINETEEN

Objective
    To review the main ideas presented in *Cry, the Beloved Country*

Activity #1
    Choose one of the review games/activities included in the packet and spend your class period as outlined there. Some materials for these activities are located in the Unit Resources section of this unit.

Activity #2
    Remind students that the Unit Test will be in the next class meeting. Stress the review of the Study Guides and their class notes as a last minute, brush-up review for homework.

REVIEW GAMES/ACTIVITIES - *Cry, the Beloved Country*

1. Ask the class to make up a unit test for *Cry, the Beloved Country*. The test should have 4 sections: matching, true/false, short answer, and essay. Students may use 1/2 period to make the test and then swap papers and use the other 1/2 class period to take a test a classmate has devised (open book). You may want to use the unit test included in this packet or take questions from the students' unit tests to formulate your own test.

2. Take 1/2 period for students to make up true and false questions (including the answers). Collect the papers and divide the class into two teams. Draw a big tic-tac-toe board on the chalk board. Make one team X and one team O. Ask questions to each side, giving each student one turn. If the question is answered correctly, that students' team's letter (X or O) is placed in the box. If the answer is incorrect, no mark is placed in the box. The object is to get three marks in a row like tic-tac-toe. You may want to keep track of the number of games won for each team.

3. Take 1/2 period for students to make up questions (true/false and short answer). Collect the questions. Divide the class into two teams. You'll alternate asking questions to individual members of teams A & B (like in a spelling bee). The question keeps going from A to B until it is correctly answered, then a new question is asked. A correct answer does not allow the team to get another question. Correct answers are +2 points; incorrect answers are -1 point.

4. Have students pair up and quiz each other from their study guides and class notes.

5. Give students a *Cry, the Beloved Country* crossword puzzle to complete.

6. Divide your class into two teams. Use the *Cry, the Beloved Country* crossword words with their letters jumbled as a word list. Student 1 from Team A faces off against Student 1 from Team B. You write the first jumbled word on the board. The first student (1A or 1B) to unscramble the word wins the chance for his/her team to score points. If 1A wins the jumble, go to student 2A and give him/her a clue. He/she must give you the correct word which matches that clue. If he/she does, Team A scores a point, and you give student 3A a clue for which you expect another correct response. Continue giving Team A clues until some team member makes an incorrect response. An incorrect response sends the game back to the jumbled-word face off, this time with students 2A and 2B. Instead of repeating giving clues to the first few students of each team, continue with the student after the one who gave the last incorrect response on the team. For example, if Team B wins the jumbled-word face-off, and student 5B gave the last incorrect answer for Team B, you would start this round of clue questions with student 6B, and so on. The team with the most points wins!

UNIT TESTS

SHORT ANSWER UNIT TEST 1 - *Cry, the Beloved Country*

I. Matching/Identify

___ 1. Gertrude   A. Stephen rented a room from her in Johannesburg.

___ 2. Absalom   B. The word for "pastor" or "reverend"

___ 3. Arthur   C. Reverend who sent for Stephen & helps him in Johannesburg

___ 4. Msimangu   D. Stephen's son who is hanged

___ 5. Vincent   E. Stephen's brother; a politician

___ 6. James   F. Stephen's sister

___ 7. Lithebe   G. Champion of the native cause; he was murdered

___ 8. Stephen   H. Priest from England who found a free lawyer

___ 9. John   I. Main character of the novel; looks for his brother, sister & son

___ 10. Umfundisi   J. Donates milk, a church, and other goods to help the native cause

II. Short Answer
1. Why did Stephen Kumalo go to Johannesburg?

2. Compare and contrast Stephen's meetings with Gertrude, John and Absalom.

3. Gertrude, John and Absalom all brought shame to Stephen Kumalo. Explain what each one did that distressed Kumalo.

Cry, the Beloved Country Short Answer Unit Test 1 Page 2

4. To what arrangement did Stephen and Absalom's girlfriend finally agree?

5. Contrast Jarvis's arrival in Johannesburg with Stephen's.

6. Why did Arthur Jarvis read about Lincoln?

7. Explain the significance of the name "Peter" for Absalom's son.

8. What gifts did Jarvis give Stephen's village?

9. What is the significance of the boy's trying to learn Zulu?

10. The last paragraph speaks of the "fear of bondage and the bondage of fear." Explain the relevance of that passage.

Cry, the Beloved Country Short Answer Unit Test 1 Page 3

III. Composition

Cry, the Beloved Country has been called, "the single most important novel in twentieth-century South African literature." Why? What is it about the book that makes it so important, so outstanding?

Cry, the Beloved Country Short Answer Unit Test 1 Page 4

IV. Vocabulary

    Listen to the vocabulary word and spell it.
    After you have spelled all the words, go back and write down the definition.

1.

2.

3.

4.

5.

6.

7.

8.

9.

10.

SHORT ANSWER UNIT TEST 2 - *Cry, the Beloved Country*

I. Matching/Identify

___ 1. Gertrude   A. Champion of the native cause; he was murdered

___ 2. Absalom   B. Stephen's brother; a politician

___ 3. Arthur   C. Main character of the novel; looks for his brother, sister & son

___ 4. Msimangu   D. Donates milk, a church, and other goods to help the native cause

___ 5. Vincent   E. The word for "pastor" or "reverend"

___ 6. James   F. Priest from England who found a free lawyer

___ 7. Lithebe   G. Stephen rented a room from her in Johannesburg.

___ 8. Stephen   H. Stephen's sister

___ 9. John   I. Reverend who sent for Stephen & helps him in Johannesburg

___ 10. Umfundisi   J. Stephen's son who is hanged

II. Short Answer

1. Paragraphs two and three in Chapter 1 sharply contrast. Explain the significance of these two paragraphs in terms of the novel's central theme.

2. "Once such a thing is opened, it cannot be shut again." Explain.

Cry, the Beloved Country Short Answer Unit Test 2 page 2

3. "The journey had begun. And now the fear back again . . . ." What fears did Kumalo have?

4. "The tragedy is not that things are broken. The tragedy is that they are not mended again." Explain what Msimangu meant. (Ch. 5)

5. What is Msimangu's one hope for his country?

6. "Cry, the beloved country, these things are not yet at an end." What "things"?

7. "There are voices crying what must be done, a hundred, a thousand voices." Chapter 12 gives several examples of what these "voices" say. What do they say?

8. "No second Johannesburg is needed upon the earth. One is enough." Explain why not.

Cry, the Beloved Country Short Answer Unit Test 2 page 3

9. "There is no applause in prison." Explain the inference regarding John Kumalo.

10. "Nothing is ever quiet except for fools." Explain.

11. What is the significance of the boy's trying to learn Zulu?

12. The last paragraph of the novel speaks of "the fear of bondage and the bondage of fear." Explain the relevance of this phrase.

Cry, the Beloved Country Short Answer Unit Test 2 page 4

III. Composition

It has been said that *Cry, the Beloved Country* is a "classic work of love and hope, courage and endurance, born of the dignity of man." Defend that statement using examples from the book.

Cry, the Beloved Country Short Answer Unit Test 2 page 5

IV. Vocabulary

    Listen to the vocabulary word and spell it.
    After you have spelled all the words, go back and write down the definition.

1.

2.

3.

4.

5.

6.

7.

8.

9.

10.

KEY: SHORT ANSWER UNIT TESTS - *Cry, the Beloved Country*

The short answer questions are taken directly from the study guides.
If you need to look up the answers, you will find them in the study guide section.

Answers to the composition questions will vary depending on your
class discussions and the level of your students.

For the vocabulary section of the test, choose ten of the
words from the vocabulary lists to read orally for your students.

The answers to the matching section of the test are below.

Answers to the matching section of the Advanced Short Answer Unit Test
are the same as for Short Answer Unit Test #2.

<u>Test #1</u>
1. F
2. D
3. G
4. C
5. H
6. J
7. A
8. I
9. E
10. B

<u>Test #2</u>
1. H
2. J
3. A
4. I
5. F
6. D
7. G
8. C
9. B
10. E

ADVANCED SHORT ANSWER UNIT TEST - *Cry, the Beloved Country*

I. Matching/Identify

___ 1. Gertrude   A. Champion of the native cause; he was murdered

___ 2. Absalom   B. Stephen's brother; a politician

___ 3. Arthur   C. Main character of the novel; looks for his brother, sister & son

___ 4. Msimangu   D. Donates milk, a church, and other goods to help the native cause

___ 5. Vincent   E. The word for "pastor" or "reverend"

___ 6. James   F. Priest from England who found a free lawyer

___ 7. Lithebe   G. Stephen rented a room from her in Johannesburg.

___ 8. Stephen   H. Stephen's sister

___ 9. John   I. Reverend who sent for Stephen & helps him in Johannesburg

___ 10. Umfundisi   J. Stephen's son who is hanged

II. Short Answer

1. Explain the significance of the title, *Cry, the Beloved Country*.

2. In what ways did Stephen Kumalo come back to his village a wiser man for having taken his trip to Johannesburg?

Cry, the Beloved Country Advanced Short Answer Unit Test page 2

3. Discuss the importance of age (youth vs. old age) in the novel.

4. What was the main theme of the novel? Use examples or evidence from the text to support your claim.

5. Each of Stephen's relatives is an individual with his/her own personality, his/her own effect on Stephen, and his/her own effect on the theme(s) of the novel. Give a brief description of each, tell the effect each has on Stephen and tell what role each plays in developing the themes of the novel.

Cry, the Beloved Country Advanced Short Answer Unit Test page 3

III. Composition

Compare and contrast The United States and South Africa on the appropriate points.

Cry, the Beloved Country Advanced Short Answer Unit Test page 4

IV. Vocabulary

Listen to the vocabulary words and write them down. After you have written down all the words, write a paragraph using all of the vocabulary words. The paragraph must in some way relate to *Cry, the Beloved Country*.

MULTIPLE CHOICE UNIT TEST 1 - *Cry, the Beloved Country*

I. Matching/Identify

___ 1. Gertrude   A. Stephen rented a room from her in Johannesburg.

___ 2. Absalom   B. The word for "pastor" or "reverend"

___ 3. Arthur   C. Reverend who sent for Stephen & helps him in Johannesburg

___ 4. Msimangu   D. Stephen's son who is hanged

___ 5. Vincent   E. Stephen's brother; a politician

___ 6. James   F. Stephen's sister

___ 7. Lithebe   G. Champion of the native cause; he was murdered

___ 8. Stephen   H. Priest from England who found a free lawyer

___ 9. John   I. Main character of the novel; looks for his brother, sister & son

___ 10. Umfundisi   J. Donates milk, a church, and other goods to help the native cause

II. Multiple Choice
1. To what was Reverend Kumalo referring when he said "...once such a thing is opened, it cannot be shut again?"
    A. He was referring to the torment in the soul of a sinner. Once a person faces up to his/her wrong doings, they (the misdeeds) can never again be denied, although they can be forgiven.
    B. He was referring to the digging of the gold mines in South Africa; the land could never be repaired.
    C. He was referring to faith. Once one opens one's heart to faith, it will always be there.
    D. He was referring to a letter he had just received. The reader would be irreversibly affected. One may also symbolically infer that once a person is made aware of a problem, he cannot turn away; the problem will not go away by itself; action must be taken.

Cry, the Beloved Country Multiple Choice Unit Test 1 Page 2

2. Which of these describes Gertrude's sickness?
    A. She is morally corrupt.
    B. She has multiple personality disorder, although no-one realizes it.
    C. She is, and has been physically ill for a long time.
    D. She is severely depressed. She has basically given up on life.

3. "The tragedy is not that things are broken. The tragedy is that they are not mended again. What does Msimangu mean?
    A. Life in the villages is becoming more difficult. Many of the young male natives are moving to the cities. The women and elderly who are left can't work the farms and keep the village going.
    B. It is bad enough that there is such injustice in South Africa although one can see how it came about. The wrong comes in that the injustices have not been eliminated since they have been recognized.
    C. The city of Johannesburg is in a state of disrepair. Many of the machines and electronic devices are broken. New buildings cannot be built, and old ones cannot be repaired, because the machinery is not working. The city government is not doing anything to correct the problem.
    D. He is referring to the family problems that Kumalo is having. He is not optimistic that they will be resolved.

4. "It is _____ that rule(s) this land." What rules the land?
    A. The weather
    B. God/religion
    C. Fear
    D. The whites

5. What is Msimangu's one hope for his country?
    A. He hopes that all of the people will become Christian.
    B. He hopes that more gold will be found to keep the country prosperous.
    C. He hopes that sickness and poverty will be eradicated in his lifetime.
    D. He hopes that the blacks and whites will work together for the good of their country.

6. "Cry, the beloved country, these things are not yet at an end." Which of the following is not being referred to in this quote from the story?
    A. "...the broken tribe..."
    B. "...the law and custom that is gone..."
    C. "...the decline of family values..."
    D. "...the man who is dead..."

Cry, the Beloved Country Multiple Choice Unit Test 1 Page 3

7. What were Arthur Jarvis' last written words?
    A. "There is a lovely road that runs from Ixopo to the hills."
    B. "Here is a chance to try out the experiment of settled mine labour."
    C. "I know what I am fighting for."
    D. "Allow me a minute."

8. In Chapter 23, the narrator expresses his opinion about Johannesburg. Which of the following quotes was used?
    A. "Gold, gold, gold. The country is going to be rich again."
    B. "No second Johannesburg is needed upon the earth. One is enough."
    C. "It is hard to be a South African. One can be born an Afrikaner, or an English-speaking South African, or a colored man, or a Zulu."
    D. "I understand better those who have died for their convictions, and have not thought it brave or noble or wonderful to die."

9. What had Arthur Jarvis written that caused his father to become "sick at heart"?
    A. "I am moved by something that is not my own, that moves me to do what is right, at whatever the cost may be."
    B. "I shall do this, not because I am noble or unselfish, but because life slips away, and because I need for the rest of my journey a star that will not play false to me."
    C. "...I learned all that a child should learn of honor and charity and generosity. But of South Africa I learned nothing at all."
    D. " But a man must get something for all his courage and foresight, and there's mental strain, too, to be taken into consideration.

10. The last paragraph of the novel speaks of "the fear of bondage and the bondage of fear." Which of the following statements is correct?
    A. The natives live in fear of bondage, and the whites live in the bondage of fear.
    B. The natives live in the bondage of fear, and the whites live in fear of bondage.
    C. Fear holds the natives captive.
    D. The natives fear freedom, the uncertain path ahead.

III. Composition
    Explain how Paton used these characters to develop his themes: Arthur Jarvis, James Jarvis, Absalom, and John. Also, tell what theme(s) they develop and how their actions relate to the theme(s).

Cry, the Beloved Country Multiple Choice Unit Test 1 Page 5

IV. Vocabulary - Match the correct definitions to the words.

____ 1. BEWILDERS   A. Marked by immorality and perversion.

____ 2. FIDELITY   B. Marked by trembling, quivering, or shaking.

____ 3. COMPELLED   C. Gather together.

____ 4. UNENDURABLE   D. Unbearable.

____ 5. WARDER   E. A statement or rhetorical discourse intended to give information about or explain difficult material

____ 6. EXPOSITION   F. Faithfulness to obligations, or duties.

____ 7. SUMMON   G. Barrenness; dreariness; hopelessness.

____ 8. ABATING   H. Lessening.

____ 9. MOULD   I. Away from the correct path or direction.

____ 10. INEVITABLE   J. A guard.

____ 11. CORRUPTED   K. General shape or form.

____ 12. DELUSION   L. Improved.

____ 13. DESOLATION   M. Impossible to avoid or prevent.

____ 14. ASTRAY   N. A false belief or opinion.

____ 15. TREMULOUS   O. Stubbornly persevering; tenaciously.

____ 16. VICIOUSLY   P. Aggressively; savagely.

____ 17. DOGGEDLY   Q. Forced to action.

____ 18. VACILLATE   R. To swing indecisively from one course of action or opinion to another.

____ 19. AMENDED   S. Ravine.

____ 20. KLOOF   T. Confuses or befuddles.

MULTIPLE CHOICE UNIT TEST 2 - *Cry, the Beloved Country*

I. Matching/Identify

___ 1. Gertrude   A. Champion of the native cause; he was murdered

___ 2. Absalom   B. Stephen's brother; a politician

___ 3. Arthur   C. Main character of the novel; looks for his brother, sister & son

___ 4. Msimangu   D. Donates milk, a church, and other goods to help the native cause

___ 5. Vincent   E. The word for "pastor" or "reverend"

___ 6. James   F. Priest from England who found a free lawyer

___ 7. Lithebe   G. Stephen rented a room from her in Johannesburg.

___ 8. Stephen   H. Stephen's sister

___ 9. John   I. Reverend who sent for Stephen & helps him in Johannesburg

___ 10. Umfundisi   J. Stephen's son who is hanged

II. Multiple Choice

1. To what was Reverend Kumalo referring when he said "...once such a thing is opened, it cannot be shut again?"
    - A. He was referring to the torment in the soul of a sinner. Once a person faces up to his/her wrong doings, they (the misdeeds) can never again be denied although they can be forgiven.
    - B. He was referring to a letter he had just received. The reader would be irreversibly affected. One may also symbolically infer that once a person is made aware of a problem, he cannot turn away; the problem will not go away by itself; action must be taken.
    - C. He was referring to faith. Once one opens one's heart to faith, it will always be there.
    - D. He was referring to the digging of the gold mines in South Africa; the land could never be repaired.

Cry, the Beloved Country Multiple Choice Unit Test 2 Page 2

2. Which of these describes Gertrude's sickness?
    A. She is, and has been physically ill for a long time. She is battling cancer. The doctors don't have the means to treat it because medical treatment for the natives almost non-existent.
    B. She has multiple personality disorder, although no-one realizes it. She has at least four distinct personalities, that range from sweet and loving to very cruel.
    C. She is morally corrupt. She makes and sells liquor, lives with prostitutes, and has been in prison.
    D. She is severely depressed. She has basically given up on life.

3. "The tragedy is not that things are broken. The tragedy is that they are not mended again. What does Msimangu mean?
    A. Life in the villages is becoming more difficult. Many of the young male natives are moving to the cities. The women and elderly who are left can't work the farms and keep the village going.
    B. He is referring to the family problems that Kumalo is having. He is not optimistic that they will be resolved.
    C. The city of Johannesburg is in a state of disrepair. Many of the machines and electronic devices are broken. New buildings cannot be built, and old ones cannot be repaired, because the machinery is not working. The city government is not doing anything to correct the problem.
    D. It is bad enough that there is such injustice in South Africa, although one can see how it came about. The wrong comes in that the injustices have not been eliminated since they have been recognized.

4. "It is _____ that rule(s) this land." What rules the land?
    A. Fear
    B. God/religion
    C. The weather
    D. The whites

5. What is Msimangu's one hope for his country?
    A. He hopes that all of the people will become Christian.
    B. He hopes that more gold will be found, to keep the country prosperous.
    C. He hopes that the blacks and whites will work together for the good of their country.
    D. He hopes that sickness and poverty will be eradicated in his lifetime.

Cry, the Beloved Country Multiple Choice Unit Test 2 Page 3

6. "Cry, the beloved country, these things are not yet at an end." Which of the following is not being referred to in this quote from the story?
    A. "...the decline of family values..."
    B. "...the law and custom that is gone..."
    C. "...the broken tribe..."
    D. "...the man who is dead..."

7. What were Arthur Jarvis' last written words?
    A. "There is a lovely road that runs from Ixopo to the hills."
    B. "Allow me a minute."
    C. "I know what I am fighting for."
    D. "Here is a chance to try out the experiment of settled mine labour."

8. In Chapter 23, the narrator expresses his opinion about Johannesburg. Which of the following quotes was used?
    A. "Gold, gold, gold. The country is going to be rich again."
    B. "It is hard to be a South African. One can be born an Afrikaner, or an English-speaking South African, or a colored man, or a Zulu."
    C. "No second Johannesburg is needed upon the earth. One is enough."
    D. "I understand better those who have died for their convictions, and have not thought it brave or noble or wonderful to die."

9. What had Arthur Jarvis written that caused his father to become "sick at heart"?
    A. "...I learned all that a child should learn of honor and charity and generosity. But of South Africa I learned nothing at all."
    B. "I shall do this, not because I am noble or unselfish, but because life slips away, and because I need for the rest of my journey a star that will not play false to me."
    C. "I am moved by something that is not my own, that moves me to do what is right, at whatever the cost may be."
    D. " But a man must get something for all his courage and foresight, and there's mental strain, too, to be taken into consideration.

10. The last paragraph of the novel speaks of "the fear of bondage and the bondage of fear." Which of the following statements is correct?
    A. Fear holds the natives captive.
    B. The natives live in the bondage of fear, and the whites live in fear of bondage.
    C. The natives live in fear of bondage, and the whites live in the bondage of fear.
    D. The natives fear freedom, the uncertain path ahead.

III. Composition

What was the point of *Cry, the Beloved Country*? Explain how the author used the characters and events in the story to deliver his main message.

Cry, the Beloved Country Multiple Choice Unit Test 2 Page 5

IV. Vocabulary - Match the correct definitions to the words.

____ 1. PARSON   A. A rural village.

____ 2. ARRAY   B. Work; painful effort; toil.

____ 3. ABATING   C. A false belief or opinion.

____ 4. LINGO   D. To split with a sharp instrument.

____ 5. BRACKEN   E. Lessening.

____ 6. TRAVAIL   F. To fill with rapture or delight.

____ 7. AMENDED   G. Unbearable.

____ 8. MUNICIPALITY H. Improved.

____ 9. KLOOF   I. To remain in place.

____ 10. DELUSION   J. Forced to action.

____ 11. COMPELLED   K. Hidden; not clearly understood.

____ 12. ABIDE   L. Display.

____ 13. UNENDURABLE M. A member of the clergy, especially a Protestant minister.

____ 14. CONVEY   N. To communicate or make known.

____ 15. PILGRIMAGE   O. Ravine.

____ 16. ENRAPT   P. Language.

____ 17. CLEAVE   Q. Suited to one's needs or nature; agreeable.

____ 18. OBSCURE   R. A political unit, such as a city or town, incorporated for local self-government.

____ 19. CONGENIAL   S. A widespread, often weedy fern.

____ 20. KRAAL   T. A long journey or search.

ANSWER SHEET - *Cry, the Beloved Country*
Multiple Choice Unit Tests

I. Matching
1. ___
2. ___
3. ___
4. ___
5. ___
6. ___
7. ___
8. ___
9. ___
10. ___

II. Multiple Choice
1. ___
2. ___
3. ___
4. ___
5. ___
6. ___
7. ___
8. ___
9. ___
10. ___

IV. Vocabulary
1. ___
2. ___
3. ___
4. ___
5. ___
6. ___
7. ___
8. ___
9. ___
10. ___
11. ___
12. ___
13. ___
14. ___
15. ___
16. ___
17. ___
18. ___
19. ___
20. ___

ANSWER KEY - *Cry, the Beloved Country*
Multiple Choice Unit Tests

Answers to Unit Test 1 are in the left column. Answers to Unit Test 2 are in the right column.

I. Matching	II. Multiple Choice	IV. Vocabulary
1. F H	1. D B	1. T M
2. D J	2. A C	2. F L
3. G A	3. B D	3. Q E
4. C I	4. C A	4. D P
5. H F	5. D C	5. J S
6. J D	6. C A	6. E B
7. A G	7. D B	7. C H
8. I C	8. B C	8. H R
9. E B	9. C A	9. K O
10. B E	10. A C	10. M C
		11. A J
		12. N I
		13. G G
		14. I N
		15. B T
		16. P F
		17. O D
		18. R K
		19. L Q
		20. S A

UNIT RESOURCE MATERIALS

BULLETIN BOARD IDEAS - *Cry, the Beloved Country*

1. Save one corner of the board for the best of students' *Cry, the Beloved Country* writing assignments.

2. Take one of the word search puzzles from the extra activities packet and with a marker copy it over in a large size on the bulletin board. Write the clue words to find to one side. Invite students prior to and after class to find the words and circle them on the bulletin board.

3. Write several of the most significant quotations from the book onto the board on brightly colored paper.

4. Make a bulletin board listing the vocabulary words for this unit. As you complete sections of the novel and discuss the vocabulary for each section, write the definitions on the bulletin board. (If your board is one students face frequently, it will help them learn the words.)

5. Place a map of Africa on the board. Highlight South Africa, and place a big red star on the cities that are mentioned in *Cry, the Beloved Country*.

6. Title the board BLACK, WHITE AND GRAY: THE PATH TO FREEDOM AND EQUALITY. Post articles and pictures relating to the struggle for racial equality, especially in South Africa.

7. Title the board LIVING WITH THE LAND. Post pictures and articles about farming techniques and pictures showing good lands and barren lands.

8. Title the board CRY, THE BELOVED COUNTRY: "IT IS FEAR THAT RULES THIS LAND." Post pictures and articles showing crime and scenes in which the "white" government's power is "threatened" (by protests, for example).

EXTRA ACTIVITIES

One of the difficulties in teaching a novel is that all students don't read at the same speed. One student who likes to read may take the book home and finish it in a day or two. Sometimes a few students finish the in-class assignments early. The problem, then, is finding suitable extra activities for students.

The best thing I've found is to keep a little library in the classroom. For this unit on *Cry, the Beloved Country*, you might check out from the school library other related books and articles about the civil rights movement, the history of South Africa, mining, tribal life, Lincoln, current events in South Africa, Alan Paton, or articles of criticism about *Cry, the Beloved Country*.

Other things you may keep on hand are puzzles. We have made some relating directly to *Cry, the Beloved Country* for you. Feel free to duplicate them.

Some students may like to draw. You might devise a contest or allow some extra-credit grade for students who draw characters or scenes from *Cry, the Beloved Country*. Note, too, that if the students do not want to keep their drawings you may pick up some extra bulletin board materials this way. If you have a contest and you supply the prize (a CD or something like that perhaps), you could, possibly, make the drawing itself a non-returnable entry fee.

The pages which follow contain games, puzzles and worksheets. The keys, when appropriate, immediately follow the puzzle or worksheet. There are two main groups of activities: one group for the unit; that is, generally relating to the *Cry, the Beloved Country* text, and another group of activities related strictly to the *Cry, the Beloved Country* vocabulary.

Directions for these games, puzzles and worksheets are self-explanatory. The object here is to provide you with extra materials you may use in any way you choose.

MORE ACTIVITIES - *Cry, the Beloved Country*

1. Pick a chapter or scene with a great deal of dialogue and have the students act it out on a stage. (Perhaps you could assign various scenes to different groups of students so more than one scene could be acted and more students could participate.)

2. Have students design a book cover (front and back and inside flaps) for *Cry, the Beloved Country*.

3. Have students design a bulletin board (ready to be put up, not just sketched) for *Cry, the Beloved Country*.

4. Use some of the related topics mentioned earlier for an in-class library as topics for guest speakers.

5. Have students make a diary for Stephen Kumalo. They should make fifteen entries as Stephen would have made them. They should choose fifteen days (or events) which most affected his knowledge and growth as a character and make an entry for each one.

6. Have your students discuss ways (and implement them when possible) that racial relations could be improved in their own communities.

7. Have students discuss or write what it is like to be black (for black students) or white (for white) students or _____ (fill in the blank for other races of students) in relationship to the opposite race. In other words, how do black (or other minority) students feel about whites, and how do white students feel about blacks (or other minorities)?

8. James Jarvis did a great deal to help the natives of Stephen's village. Are there things your students could do to help people in your community? Have them brainstorm ideas and carry them out when possible.

9. Have a "South Africa Day" in which you have students dress in the native costumes, eat native foods, and learn about the different customs related to the different people in South Africa.

WORD SEARCH - *Cry, the Beloved Country*

All words in this list are associated with *Cry, the Beloved Country*. The words are placed backwards, forward, diagonally, up and down. The included words are listed below the word search.

```
J O H A N N E S B U R G F E A R S L A W Y E R F
R Q H L N D S M D J H E B P D M Z R I D N V C V
Q Y R A R K L Y O S D E T U D U P S E N V L X R
A J O H N C J E T U H S G E M V R G G P C S Q C
C B J C F G L J L T N L H U P F A T Q R T O S G
Q W S L A L G B I A P T A L I R U T R H S F L H
H D Z A I R W L Z R G E A B T L N N G E N V R N
B F N V L K M I S S I O N I E D T I D K G G C R
G Q M W Y O C I W B H C C R N N L Y D I J M R D
F I G M Y N M X C C P J R W I D I D Y B S Q H E
P F N N Q V Z X S H K C D C D C J W S P Q I S J
V T S B A M Y T L L A N H H L L H R Q Z Y U H K
C M E G T T N Q Z Y E E S V V O X L R P A K W J
P J R K D E I B X H R C L I W G T Y V L W J A N
J Z L P C P R V P B X T N M V A M H P B Q M K M
V A R N V I S E E S P S N Q L R J P E J E U V Y
M K I Z E F T U H S Z U L U G N A M I S M I L K
P V Q L F S K N U B C I B O O T V J F A F X Q H
M W G B S B L B N V E U H R O C C H L R F G H W
T K Y J J Y R Q K S D X J N N F D O W X V R D K
```

ABSALOM	GUILTY	LIGHTS	PETER
APPLAUSE	HANG	LINCOLN	PIMVILLE
BUS	HLABENI	LITHEBE	SHUT
CARMICHAEL	JAIL	MILK	STEPHEN
CLOTHES	JAMES	MISSION	TICKET
COUNTRY	JARVIS	MKIZE	TRAGEDY
DUBULA	JOHANNESBURG	MOUNTAIN	UMFUNDISI
ENRICH	JOHN	MSIMANGU	VINCENT
FEARS	KUMALO	NATIVES	ZULU
FOOLS	LAWYER	NDLELA	
GERTRUDE	LIES	PATON	

CROSSWORD - *Cry, the Beloved Country*

CROSSWORD CLUES - *Cry, the Beloved Country*

ACROSS
1. Stephen's sister; he finds her living in immorality
4. Mr. Jarvis's first gift to the children
8. Word for 'pastor' or 'reverend'
9. Place where Stephen meets his son
10. Cry, the beloved ___, these things are not yet at an end.
11. Absalom was sentenced to _____
12. Author
15. Taxi driver
17. A thought
18. Gertrude's new ___ symbolize putting on a new life
23. A young man stole Stephen's money for his bus ___
24. Arthur; the murdered champion of the Native cause
25. The ___'s not that things are broken. The ___ is that they are not mended again.
28. Reverend who sent for Stephen, telling him of his sister's illness
31. Absalom's attorney
34. Name for Absalom's son
36. Serviceable; having a practical use
38. Place Kumalo found a native girl Absalom had abandoned
39. Stephen's son who has become a criminal
41. Stephen has many of these as his journey begins
42. Stephen's brother, a politician
44. Partner of 'that'
46. Place of spiritual refreshment for Kumalo

DOWN
1. Verdict for Absalom
2. Preposition; 'The road climbs 7 miles into the hills, -- Carisbrooke....'
3. Tomlinson has the brains, John has the voice, but ___ has the heart.
4. Said Absalom had been stealing and was in bad company
5. Stephen's last name
6. The Natives were refusing to ride the ___ in protest of increased fares
7. Stephen rented a room from her
9. _____ Jarvis, Arthur's father. He donates things.
13. John speaks in public for their cause
14. The ___ ... fall... on the grass and stones of a country that sleeps.
16. John ___ about his son's involvement with Absalom
19. Father Vincent's gift for Absalom
20. Fear impoverishes always, while sorrow may ___.
21. Definite article
22. Priest from England who found a free lawyer for Absalom
26. The boy tries to learn this language
27. Because of the boycott, they didn't ---- the bus
29. _____ House
30. Says the police are looking for Absalom
32. There is no ___ in prison.
33. Pastor who goes to Johannesburg to find his sister (& brother & son)
35. Arthur Jarvis read about this American president
37. Nothing is ever quiet except for ____.
40. Once such a thing is opened, it cannot be --- again.
43. Possess
45. Negative response

CROSSWORD ANSWER KEY - *Cry, the Beloved Country*

MATCHING QUIZ/WORKSHEET 1 - *Cry, the Beloved Country*

____ 1. ENRICH   A. Absalom was sentenced to _____

____ 2. LITHEBE   B. Stephen's son who has become a criminal

____ 3. VINCENT   C. Author

____ 4. LIES   D. John speaks in public for their cause

____ 5. LINCOLN   E. Stephen has many of these as his journey begins

____ 6. FEARS   F. The ___ ... fall... on the grass and stones of a country that sleeps

____ 7. ABSALOM   G. Name for Absalom's son

____ 8. SHUT   H. Pastor who goes to Johannesburg to find his sister (& brother & son)

____ 9. LAWYER   I. Father Vincent's gift for Absalom

____ 10. NATIVES   J. Fear impoverishes always, while sorrow may ___

____ 11. TRAGEDY   K. Stephen rented a room from her

____ 12. JAIL   L. The ___'s not that things are broken. The ___ is that they are not mended again.

____ 13. HANG   M. Nothing is ever quiet except for ____.

____ 14. GERTRUDE   N. Once such a thing is opened, it cannot be --- again.

____ 15. UMFUNDISI   O. Priest from England who found a free lawyer for Absalom

____ 16. PATON   P. Stephen's sister; he finds her living in immorality

____ 17. FOOLS   Q. Place where Stephen meets his son

____ 18. STEPHEN   R. Arthur Jarvis read about this American president

____ 19. PETER   S. John ___ about his son's involvement with Absalom

____ 20. LIGHTS   T. Word for 'pastor' or 'reverend'

MATCHING QUIZ/WORKSHEET 2 - *Cry, the Beloved Country*

___ 1. COUNTRY   A. Stephen's last name

___ 2. LIES   B. Stephen has many of these as his journey begins

___ 3. ABSALOM   C. John speaks in public for their cause

___ 4. LINCOLN   D. Verdict for Absalom

___ 5. TRAGEDY   E. Place where Stephen meets his son

___ 6. GUILTY   F. Place Kumalo found a native girl Absalom had abandoned

___ 7. NATIVES   G. Stephen rented a room from her

___ 8. PIMVILLE   H. Author

___ 9. LITHEBE   I. Absalom was sentenced to _____

___ 10. KUMALO   J. Arthur Jarvis read about this American president

___ 11. PATON   K. John ___ about his son's involvement with Absalom

___ 12. HANG   L. Priest from England who found a free lawyer for Absalom

___ 13. ENRICH   M. Pastor who goes to Johannesburg to find his sister (& brother & son)

___ 14. ZULU   N. The boy tries to learn this language

___ 15. FEARS   O. Cry, the beloved ___, these things are not yet at an end.

___ 16. STEPHEN   P. _____ Jarvis, Arthur's father. He donates things.

___ 17. JAMES   Q. Stephen's son who has become a criminal

___ 18. VINCENT   R. Reverend who sent for Stephen, telling him of his sister's illness

___ 19. MSIMANGU   S. Fear impoverishes always, while sorrow may ___.

___ 20. JAIL   T. The ___'s not that things are broken. The ___ is that they are not mended again.

KEY: MATCHING QUIZ/WORKSHEETS - *Cry, the Beloved Country*

Worksheet 1	Worksheet 2
1. J	1. O
2. K	2. K
3. O	3. Q
4. S	4. J
5. R	5. T
6. E	6. D
7. B	7. C
8. N	8. F
9. I	9. G
10. D	10. A
11. L	11. H
12. Q	12. I
13. A	13. S
14. P	14. N
15. T	15. B
16. C	16. M
17. M	17. P
18. H	18. L
19. G	19. R
20. F	20. E

JUGGLE LETTER REVIEW GAME CLUE SHEET - *Cry, the Beloved Country*

SCRAMBLED	WORD	CLUE
LASMOBA	ABSALOM	Stephen's son who has become a criminal
PULPASEA	APPLAUSE	There is no ___ in prison.
SUB	BUS	The natives were refusing to ride the ___ in protest of increased fares
CHALERMICA	CARMICHAEL	Absalom's attorney
SLOTHEC	CLOTHES	Gertrude's new ___ symbolize putting on a new life
TOUNYRC	COUNTRY	Cry, the beloved ___, these things are not yet at an end.
BLUUAD	DUBULA	Tomlinson has the brains, John has the voice, but ___ has the heart.
CRIHEN	ENRICH	Fear impoverishes always, while sorrow may ___.
REAFS	FEARS	Stephen has many of these as his journey begins
SOLOF	FOOLS	Nothing is ever quiet except for ___.
ERGDTUER	GERTRUDE	Stephen's sister; he finds her living in immorality
ILYGUT	GUILTY	Verdict for Absalom
GAHN	HANG	Absalom was sentenced to ___
BINELAH	HLABENI	Taxi driver
LAJI	JAIL	Place where Stephen meets his son
SAJEM	JAMES	Jarvis, Arthur's father. He donates things.
IVRJSA	JARVIS	Arthur; the murdered champion of the native cause
NEUGSBHNORJA	JOHANNESBURG	City Stephen goes to find his sister
HJNO	JOHN	Stephen's brother, a politician
ULKAOM	KUMALO	Stephen's last name
WAYELR	LAWYER	Father Vincent's gift for Absalom
SLEI	LIES	John ___ about his son's involvement with Absalom
GITSHL	LIGHTS	The ___ ... fall... on the grass and stones of a country that sleeps.
LONNILC	LINCOLN	Arthur Jarvis read about this American president
BILTEHE	LITHEBE	Stephen rented a room from her
LIMK	MILK	Mr. Jarvis's first gift to the children
SISMONI	MISSION	___ House
ZKMEI	MKIZE	Said Absalom had been stealing and was in bad company
ONAMTNIU	MOUNTAIN	Place of spiritual refreshment for Kumalo
GMNASMUI	MSIMANGU	Reverend who sent for Stephen, telling him of his sister's illness
ASVTNIE	NATIVES	John speaks in public for their cause
ELLAND	NDLELA	Says the police are looking for Absalom
POTAN	PATON	Author
PTEER	PETER	Name for Absalom's son

ELVPMIIL	PIMVILLE	Place Kumalo found a native girl Absalom had abandoned
HUTS	SHUT	Once such a thing is opened, it cannot be --- again.
PEETHNS	STEPHEN	Pastor who goes to Johannesburg to find his sister & brother & son)
KITCTE	TICKET	A young man stole Stephen's money for his bus ___
GRADTEY	TRAGEDY	The ___'s not that things are broken. The ___ is that they are not mended again.
FIDNUSMUI	UMFUNDISI	Word for 'pastor' or 'reverend'
CINVTEN	VINCENT	Priest from England who found a free lawyer for Absalom
UUZL	ZULU	The boy tries to learn this language

VOCABULARY RESOURCE MATERIALS

VOCABULARY WORD SEARCH - *Cry, the Beloved Country*

All words in this list are associated with *Cry, the Beloved Country* with an emphasis on the vocabulary words chosen for study in the text. The words are placed backwards, forward, diagonally, up and down. The included words are listed below.

```
K R A A L M S D B E R E A V E M E N T D S Y F D
Y P Z E S I O U P R Y E D B V W G D E Y E O W Q
T F Z Z T R N U B D A L X V I Y W H U V O L C D
S P H L K A S G L S U C L P Y D S R N L A W L P
T R A V A I L Y O D I B K A O I E O K K E E P N
V W E R M I K L M D Y D I E N S C L B L R R L J
X F R D N G N G I P E Y I O N O I E B U O L P C
U A C R L E N E Q C O S T E U C I T C A C R L T
Y N S R E I T V G P A S O G S S O S I A P V R Z
R L E O N P W A I N A V I L C U B M I O N L Z Y
I L N N M O E E C C O R T U A O M G P V N E U V
M R U E D B I N B C I C S R M T R M R E O Z M C
A C R W L U R T T O O A O E D I R O A L R F D
R S Z I A L R E A P Y M U B N M E O U N T L P J
P E T Q T R U A C R E C P S A Q U L N P Y I E D
L J V R B A D S B N I H O L L T Q L U Z T C F D
Q L X E A W T E D L Z P V T I Y I Y O S Y E S Y
D Q F L R Y M E R S E C S Q T C Y N B U I R D Z
Z S Q Y G I D I N E V I T A B L E W G B S O X Y
F P E R P L E X E D L P E R M I S S I B L E N D
```

ABATING	CONGENIAL	KLOOF	SOMBRE
ABIDE	CONVEY	KRAAL	SUBSIDIES
ACCOMPLICES	CORRUPTED	LINGO	SULLENLY
AMENDED	CULPABLE	LORRY	SUMMON
ARRAY	CUNNING	MENACE	SYMPOSIUM
ASPIRATION	DELL	MOULD	TIERS
ASTONISHED	DELUSION	OBSCURE	TRAVAIL
ASTRAY	DESOLATION	PARSON	TREMULOUS
BEREAVEMENT	DUBIOUS	PERMISSIBLE	UNENDURABLE
BEWILDERS	ENRAPT	PERPLEXED	VACILLATE
BOYCOTT	EXPOSITION	PRELUDE	VICIOUSLY
BRACKEN	GRATIFY	PROVISIONALLY	WARDER
CLEAVE	INEVITABLE	REPENT	
COMPELLED	IRRITATE	REVERIE	

VOCABULARY CROSSWORD - *Cry, the Beloved Country*

VOCABULARY CROSSWORD CLUES - *Cry, the Beloved Country*

ACROSS
1. A strong, irresistible force on; exerted
6. General shape or form
8. Hidden; not clearly understood
12. Prefix meaning against
14. Suited to one's needs or nature; agreeable
15. Away from the correct path or direction
17. The space between two things
18. A standard; a set of rules; --- of ethics; a moral ----
19. A small, secluded, wooded valley
20. To remain in place
22. An action
23. Nothing is ever quiet except for ____
24. Absalom was sentenced to _____
25. A motor truck
26. Place where Stephen meets his son
29. Affirmative answer
30. Depend on
31. Willing to do a service or favor for
35. To fill with rapture or delight
36. One of a series of rows placed one above another
37. To abstain from using, buying, or dealing with as a form of protest
40. Anger
41. Indefinite article
42. Taking advantage of people or a situation for monetary gain
43. Acquire
45. Dark; gloomy; serious; grave
47. Ravine
48. Showing a brooding ill humor
49. Fear impoverishes always, while sorrow may __

DOWN
1. Subtle; deceitful
2. A political unit, such as a city or town, incorporated for local self-government
3. Stephen to Absalom
4. The Natives were refusing to ride the ___ in protest of increased fares
5. A rural village
6. A possible danger; a threat
7. Unbearable
9. Confuses or befuddles
10. To split with a sharp instrument
11. To please or satisfy
13. A guard
16. Work; painful effort; toil
21. A statement or rhetorical discourse intended to give information about or explain difficult material
23. Stephen has many of these as his journey begins
25. Language
27. Marked by immorality and perversion
28. Lessening
32. To feel such regret for past conduct as to change one's mind regarding it
33. Annoy; bother
34. Stephen's brother, a politician
37. A widespread, often weedy fern
38. A member of the clergy, especially a Protestant minister
39. To communicate or make known
44. Mr. Jarvis's first gift to the children
46. Belonging to me

VOCABULARY CROSSWORD ANSWER KEY - *Cry, the Beloved Country*

VOCABULARY WORKSHEET 1 - *Cry, the Beloved Country*

____ 1. A strong, irresistible force on; exerted.
    A. Compelled   B. Prelude   C. Vagabonds   D. Enrapt

____ 2. A long journey or search.
    A. Provisionally   B. Culpable   C. Pilgrimage   D. Irritate

____ 3. Temporarily.
    A. Prelude   B. Provisionally   C. Hindrance   D. Abide

____ 4. Annoy; bother.
    A. Compelled   B. Exploitation   C. Kloof   D. Irritate

____ 5. Unsure of how to act or proceed; undecided.
    A. Aspiration   B. Bracken   C. Reproachfully   D. Irresolute

____ 6. Stubbornly persevering; tenaciously.
    A. Vacillate   B. Doggedly   C. Hindrance   D. Viciously

____ 7. A motor truck.
    A. Abide   B. Lorry   C. Parson   D. Obliging

____ 8. To communicate or make known.
    A. Kloof   B. Convey   C. Kraal   D. Corrupted

____ 9. To abstain from using, buying, or dealing with as a form of protest.
    A. Boycott   B. Irresolute   C. Self-denunciation   D. Abating

____ 10. To fill with rapture or delight.
    A. Prelude   B. Dubious   C. Perplexed   D. Enrapt

____ 11. To feel such regret for past conduct as to change one's mind regarding it.
    A. Vacillate   B. Repent   C. Fidelity   D. Perplexed

____ 12. To please or satisfy.
    A. Self-denunciation   B. Accomplices   C. Exposition   D. Gratify

____ 13. Taking advantage of people or a situation for monetary gain.
    A. Constraint   B. Prelude   C. Exploitation   D. Compelled

____ 14. To remain in place.
    A. Delusion   B. Convey   C. Reproachfully   D. Abide

____ 15. Impossible to avoid or prevent.
    A. Fidelity   B. Self-denunciation   C. Inevitable   D. Subsidies

____ 16. An impediment; something that gets in the way.
    A. Permissible   B. Lorry   C. Kloof   D. Hindrance

____ 17. Hidden; not clearly understood.
    A. Hindrance   B. Obscure   C. Incorruptible   D. Compelled

____ 18. suited to one's needs or nature; agreeable.
    A. Summon   B. Aspiration   C. Delusion   D. Congenial

____ 19. A meeting or conference for discussion of a topic.
    A. Symposium   B. Incorruptible   C. Reverie   D. Parson

____ 20. Marked by trembling, quivering, or shaking.
    A. Tremulous   B. Amended   C. Vagabonds   D. Lorry

VOCABULARY WORKSHEET 2 - *Cry, the Beloved Country*

____ 1. REPROACHFULLY

____ 2. MUNICIPALITY

____ 3. TREMULOUS

____ 4. IRRITATE

____ 5. REPENT

____ 6. VICIOUSLY

____ 7. MENACE

____ 8. NEGROPHILE

____ 9. ASPIRATION

____ 10. INEVITABLE

____ 11. ENRAPT

____ 12. KRAAL

____ 13. CONGENIAL

____ 14. BEWILDERS

____ 15. KLOOF

____ 16. GRATIFY

____ 17. SELF-DENUNCIATION

____ 18. EXPOSITION

____ 19. COMPELLED

____ 20. INCORRUPTIBLE

A. A statement or rhetorical discourse intended to give information about or explain difficult material

B. Self-accusation; self-condemnation.

C. Expressing blame.

D. Annoy; bother.

E. To fill with rapture or delight.

F. Exerted a strong, irresistible force on

G. A political unit, such as a city or town, incorporated for local self-government.

H. Aggressively; savagely.

I. Incapable of being swayed to do anything immoral, illegal, or unethical

J. Impossible to avoid or prevent.

K. Confuses or befuddles.

L. A possible danger; a threat.

M. Ravine.

N. A rural village.

O. A strong desire for high achievement; ambition.

P. One friendly to Negros and their interests.

Q. To feel such regret for past conduct as to change one's mind regarding it.

R. To please or satisfy.

S. Marked by trembling, quivering, or shaking.

T. Suited to one's needs or nature; agreeable.

KEY: VOCABULARY WORKSHEETS - *Cry, the Beloved Country*

Worksheet 1	Worksheet 2
1. A	1. C
2. C	2. G
3. B	3. S
4. D	4. D
5. D	5. Q
6. B	6. H
7. B	7. L
8. B	8. P
9. A	9. O
10. D	10. J
11. B	11. E
12. D	12. N
13. C	13. T
14. D	14. K
15. C	15. M
16. D	16. R
17. B	17. B
18. D	18. A
19. A	19. F
20. A	20. I

VOCABULARY JUGGLE LETTER REVIEW GAME CLUES - *Cry, the Beloved Country*

SCRAMBLED	WORD	CLUE
FLOOK	KLOOF	Ravine
KNRAECB	BRACKEN	A widespread, often weedy fern
ROLYR	LORRY	A motor truck
RAALK	KRAAL	A rural village
GGIMRPALIE	PILGRIMAGE	A long journey or search
EDLL	DELL	A small, secluded, wooded valley
DEFYITLI	FIDELITY	Faithfulness to obligations, or duties
IYLAPTCINUMI	MUNICIPALITY	A political unit, such as a city or town, incorporated for local self-government
NELLYUSL	SULLENLY	Showing a brooding ill humor
NUCNGNI	CUNNING	Subtle; deceitful
DELELPMOC	COMPELLED	A strong, irresistible force on; exerted
FGYTAIR	GRATIFY	To please or satisfy
XNOIIOTSEP	EXPOSITION	A statement or rhetorical discourse intended to give information about or explain difficult material
TYTOOCB	BOYCOTT	To abstain from using, buying, or dealing with as a form of protest
UOSRTERELI	IRRESOLUTE	Unsure of how to act or proceed; undecided
DESHINTOSA	ASTONISHED	To fill with sudden wonder or amazement
OPRURCETD	CORRUPTED	Marked by immorality and perversion
SRDEBWEIL	BEWILDERS	Confuses or befuddles
LAATRVI	TRAVAIL	Work; painful effort; toil
RONPAS	PARSON	A member of the clergy, especially a Protestant minister
BOCRUES	OBSCURE	Hidden; not clearly understood
NAESOOITDL	DESOLATION	Barrenness; dreariness; hopelessness
POMCALICECS	ACCOMPLICES	Those who aid a lawbreaker in a criminal act
NECMEA	MENACE	A possible danger; a threat
LICAVATEL	VACILLATE	To swing indecisively from one course of action or opinion to another
SUUBDOI	DUBIOUS	Doubtful
MUMPOSISY	SYMPOSIUM	A meeting or conference for discussion of a topic
YASRAT	ASTRAY	Away from the correct path or direction
SONGBADAV	VAGABONDS	People without a permanent home who move from place to place
VEELAC	CLEAVE	To split with a sharp instrument
TRAPNE	ENRAPT	To fill with rapture or delight

RRDAEW	WARDER	A guard
MOSMNU	SUMMON	Gather together
DENNULEABUR	UNENDURABLE	Unbearable
GOGLEYDD	DOGGEDLY	Stubbornly persevering; tenaciously
CHLUFYEPOARLR	REPROACHFULLY	Expressing blame
DEEDMAN	AMENDED	Improved
TITIRARE	IRRITATE	Annoy; bother
TERENP	REPENT	To feel such regret for past conduct as to change one's mind regarding it
DLUMO	MOULD	General shape or form
NOCEYV	CONVEY	To communicate or make known
HADSVANRE	VERANDAHS	A porch or balcony, usually roofed and often partly enclosed, extending along the outside of a building
LIONNEGCA	CONGENIAL	Suited to one's needs or nature; agreeable
LYANORPIISVLO	PROVISIONALLY	Temporarily
GONLI	LINGO	Language
LABLETCEUNI	INELUCTABLE	Not to be avoided or escaped; inevitable
SISIMERPLEB	PERMISSIBLE	Permitted; allowable
TOILETPOXNIA	EXPLOITATION	Taking advantage of people or a situation for monetary gain
LABETIEVNI	INEVITABLE	Impossible to avoid or prevent
SESIDIBUS	SUBSIDIES	Monetary assistance granted by a government
STEIR	TIERS	A series of rows placed one above another
COINURBITELPR	INCORRUPTIBLE	Incapable of being swayed to do anything immoral, illegal, or unethical
BLAPLUCE	CULPABLE	Deserving of blame or censure as being wrong
HOGNRELIEP	NEGROPHILE	One friendly to Negroes and their interests
RIPSAAINOT	ASPIRATION	A strong desire for high achievement; ambition
NNEICRADH	HINDRANCE	An impediment; something that gets in the way
NAINSOCRTT	CONSTRAINT	Awkwardness
SOULRETUM	TREMULOUS	Marked by trembling, quivering, or shaking
DIBAE	ABIDE	To remain in place
REPDULE	PRELUDE	Introduction
EXERPEPDL	PERPLEXED	Confused or troubled with uncertainty or doubt
GINGBLOI	OBLIGING	Willing to do a service or favor for
SUDLIONE	DELUSION	A false belief or opinion
EERREVI	REVERIE	Daydream

RAARY	ARRAY	Display
GINTAAB	ABATING	Lessening
REEEETVABMN	BEREAVEMENT	Grief over someone's death
MERSOB	SOMBRE	Dark; gloomy; serious; grave
MOCLELEPD	COMPELLED	Forced to action